Luther's Revolution

Princeton Theological Monograph Series

K. C. Hanson, Charles M. Collier, D. Christopher Spinks,
and Robin Parry, Series Editors

Recent volumes in the series:

Neal J. Anthony
*Cross Narratives: Martin Luther's Christology
and the Location of Redemption*

Michael S. Whiting
*Luther in English: The Influence of His Theology of Law
and Gospel on Early English Evangelicals (1525–1535)*

Caryn D. Riswold
Coram Deo: Human Life in the Vision of God

Jens Zimmermann
*Being Human, Becoming Human:
Dietrich Bonhoeffer and Social Thought*

Eric G. Flett
*Persons, Powers, and Pluralities:
Toward a Trinitarian Theology of Culture*

Myk Habets
Trinitarian Theology after Barth

Nikolaus Ludwig von Zinzendorf
*Christian Life and Witness:
Count Zinzendorf's 1738 Berlin Speeches*

Luther's Revolution

The Political Dimensions of Martin Luther's Universal Priesthood

Nathan Montover

☙PICKWICK *Publications* · Eugene, Oregon

LUTHER'S REVOLUTION
The Political Dimensions of Martin Luther's Universal Priesthood

Princeton Theological Monograph Series 161

Copyright © 2011 Nathan Montover. All rights reserved. Except for brief quotations in critical publications or reviews, no part of this book may be reproduced in any manner without prior written permission from the publisher. Write: Permissions, Wipf and Stock Publishers, 199 W. 8th Ave., Suite 3, Eugene, OR 97401.

Pickwick Publications
An Imprint of Wipf and Stock Publishers
199 W. 8th Ave., Suite 3
Eugene, OR 97401

www.wipfandstock.com

ISBN 13: 978-1-60899-993-4

Cataloging-in-Publication data:

Montover, Nathan.

    Luther's revolution : the political dimensions of Martin Luther's universal priesthood / Nathan Montover.

    Princeton Theological Monograph Series 161

    x + 154 p. ; 23 cm. Includes bibliographical references.

    ISBN 13: 978-1-60899-993-4

    1. Luther, Martin, 1483–1546—Views on universal priesthood. 2. Priesthood, Universal—History of doctrines. 3. Christianity and politics. 4. Church and state. I. Title. II. Series.

BT767.5 M85 2011

Manufactured in the U.S.A.

To my sons
Christian, Jacob, and Philip

Contents

Acknowledgments / ix

Introduction / 1

1. Historiographical Assumptions / 7
2. Biographical Appraisals of the Political Dimensions of Luther's Universal Priesthood / 15
3. A Consideration of Luther's Body of Work on the Topic of the Universal Priesthood / 37
4. The Social and Political Context of Papal Claims of Temporal Authority / 66
5. Luther's Response to Claims of Papal Authority in "To the Christian Nobility of the German Nation" / 102
6. Conclusions and Trajectories for Further Studies / 138

Bibliography / 151

Acknowledgments

I would like to express my gratitude to all the saints at St. James Lutheran Church, where I served as pastor while writing this book. I would also like to thank all my students at Augustana College, Rock Island, Illinois, who unknowingly allowed me to explore the ideas expressed in this book during our many conversations in and out of class.

A word of gratitude is also owed to Dr. Kurt Hendel, Dr. Vitor Westhelle, and Dr. Mark Swanson who read and re-read drafts of this book when it was still a mere dissertation.

Special thanks is owed to my friend, and colleague, Pr. Bill Bernau who helped me immensely by proofreading and editing my work.

Finally, I wish to recognize and thank my wife, Sarah, and our sons, Christian, Jacob, and Philip, who endured many hours without me so that I could work on this project.

Introduction

A YEAR AFTER MY ORDINATION AS A LUTHERAN PASTOR I TOOK A TRIP with two friends to Germany in order to "discover" Martin Luther. We traveled to his birthplace. We also made the obligatory stop at the Wartburg castle. However, I held on to the belief that it would be in the city of Wittenberg that I would finally make the connection to Luther that I had been longing to experience.

Our first stop in Wittenberg was at the castle church where we looked at the door where Luther presumably nailed his 95 theses (only to discover that it wasn't the *real* door). We then went to the city church where we were able to ascend the pulpit that Luther would have preached from (only to discover that it wasn't the *real* pulpit).

I was struck at how little the place moved me. I expected to find a deep connection to Luther but all I ended up with was a set of postcards printed with the artwork of Lucas Cranach that adorns the altar in the city church. As I was ready to leave the church—somewhat disappointed—a choir from an American Lutheran college arrived and began to sing.

I am not a person prone to tears, but when that choir began to sing the church became alive and full of meaning and the mystical connection to Luther for which I had been searching was finally made. My eyes and my heart welled up.

It was not the building or the history, but rather the people who made all the difference. Real voices singing real songs made the place real for me. I had not "discovered" Luther, but I did become more aware of his Reformation rooted not in places or history, but people.

I still have those postcards that I bought in the city church—they are perched on some books next to me as I write these words. One of the cards depicts a grand procession of vested clerics and monks attending to some sort of holy gathering. Behind them stands Luther, surrounded by other reformers. They are all farming. Once again I am reminded that Luther's Reformation was not simply about places and history.

I

It was fundamentally about people and their relationships to one another; people and their relationship to God.

From these experiences—informed by thoughtful and extensive reading of Luther's writings—it has become apparent to me that one cannot depict Luther nor understand his evangelical theology and the Reformation movement it informed, without grasping the reality that Luther was interested in how Christianity impacts the daily lives of believers and the structures that govern their lives and attend to their faith.

Luther articulated a theology that had deep and profound implications for how believers comprehended the work of God in Christ. However, his thinking also had implications for how social order was to be determined and how political authority was to be understood in relation to sacred authority.

To put it simply, Luther's theological reformation was also a political reformation with implications for the structuring of the temporal world. In fact, perhaps the term reformation is not sufficient. Perhaps Luther's political thought was revolutionary.

Mainstream scholars have been reluctant to allow such claims to be made. As evidenced in well-known biographies of Luther, the Reformer is portrayed as politically conservative. He also tends to be portrayed as politically naive. The experts have spoken; Luther was not a political figure. He was a brilliant monk who was caught up in political realities in which he was not fundamentally interested.

I wish to present research that confronts the long-held assumptions about the political dimensions of Luther's thought. It is my intention to present the reader with a case study to make my point that Luther's articulation of evangelical theology at times functioned as a means of transforming the church and the world—or to use more modern language, church and state, and that Luther was fundamentally interested in the structures of the world.

For my case study I have chosen to examine Luther's doctrine of the priesthood of all believers as it was articulated in the 1520 treatise "To the Christian Nobility of the German Nation." The fact that the political dimensions of "To the Christian Nobility of the German Nation" have been oft overlooked by scholars is self-evident. In the introduction to the English version of "Temporal Authority: To What Extent It Should Be Obeyed" (1523), the editor claims that the treatise, "is the first ethical defense of temporal government against the prevailing Roman Catholic concept that the church is the source of all earthly authority."[1] Obviously the editor had overlooked "To the Christian Nobility of the German Nation," written three years earlier.

In "To the Christian Nobility of the German Nation" Luther attacks the notion of papal authority and calls on temporal authorities to reform the church. He challenges the ancient notion that the papacy has authority over temporal leaders. He then attaches himself to a tradition of German grievances against papal abuses in temporal matters by reiterating long-held complaints (*gravamina*) and proposes a reform program that will radically change the medieval understanding of the church and the secular order.

I will argue that Luther's doctrine of the priesthood of all believers is an example of how Luther engaged in a very real and robust attempt to reshape both the ecclesiastical and temporal structures of his day. Thus, the universal priesthood cannot be considered exclusively as a doctrine aimed at reforming the structures of the church, but must be considered as a part of the way Luther understood the need to change the structures of the temporal world as well. I will also argue that this reality has been silenced by scholars of the Reformation.

In the first chapter of this work I will present my methodological approach to Luther and the examination of his universal priesthood. I contend that Luther's universal priesthood has been inadequately examined due to a silence that has been created by contemporary scholars. Building on the work of Michel-Rolph Trouillot, I will explore the impact of how history is silenced by omissions. In the case of Luther, the oft-held assumption is that his theology did not specifically address issues of social justice and systemic change in the temporal realm. For most scholars Luther's only contribution to the understanding of the political and temporal realm is to be found in his "doctrine" of the two governances. Certainly his doctrine of the universal priesthood is not considered to be evidence of Luther's desire to reform the political as well as the ecclesiastical realms.

What is missing from this assessment of Luther, and its continuation by scholars of early modern history, is the hard evidence that Luther was not only engaged in attacking temporal structures but that his attack was seen as an obvious threat by the ultimate temporal es-

1. Luther, *Luther's Works*, Hereafter cited as LW. LW 45:80.

tablishment, the church—impacted by claims of temporal authority made by the pope. By telling this story, which is in reality not all that controversial, one gives voice to a silenced aspect of Luther's life and the development of evangelical doctrine.

I will also point out the prophetic and revolutionary aspects of Luther's theology by utilizing definitions provided by Cornel West in his book *Prophesy Deliverance!* West defines prophesy as the act of identifying concrete evils. This comes about through a movement from abstract thought about God and God's will in the world into "concrete enactments of existential and political struggles with no human guarantee for ultimate victory."[2]

Luther's letter to the Christian nobility fits with West's understanding of prophetic utterance. Luther identifies a specific evil, the walls erected to protect the papacy from reform, and imagines a way to challenge those walls at their very foundations. Will his program work? Will emperor and prince alike take upon themselves the mantle of priest and reform the church? Who knows? What matters is that Luther imagined the possibilities and presented a framework for making that dream a reality.

Chapter two will contain a review of research conclusions on Luther's doctrine of the universal priesthood as presented by contemporary biographers and scholars. The first task is to challenge the long-standing assumption that Luther articulated his understanding of the universal priesthood as a doctrine related primarily to the office of ministry. Certainly this was a part of his understanding of the doctrine, but to assume that this is the foremost issue is to ignore the context of one of his most well-known treatises on the subject. In order to accomplish this task I will examine a variety of biographies and works which attempt to distill Luther's theology and tell the story of his life's work.

In the case of Luther's development of the doctrine of the priesthood of all believers, the facts are often presented in this way: after discovering the core of the gospel of justification by grace through faith alone, Luther applied that doctrine to the structures of the church and developed the doctrine of the priesthood of all believers for the sake of better defining the office of ministry and the nature of the church. This fact is correct, but insufficient. This view is presented almost exclusively in the conversations concerning the context behind Luther's decision

---

2. West, *Prophesy Deliverance*, 6.

to articulate a doctrine of the universal priesthood. My contention will be that Luther most certainly applied this doctrine to his understanding of the role of the temporal powers and thus intentionally used the doctrine as a way of visioning a new temporal structure.

In chapter three I will explore the ways in which Luther understood the universal priesthood throughout his career as a reformer. A study of a variety of texts is needed in order to place "To the Christian Nobility of the German Nation" in its proper theological and historical context. Luther oftentimes wrote of the doctrine within the context of simple ecclesiastical and sacramental reforms. Much of what is assumed about Luther's understanding of the universal priesthood by biographers and theologians alike applies to some of what Luther wrote on the subject. Yet, "To the Christian Nobility of the German Nation," when studied alongside Luther's other writing on the universal priesthood, stands in stark contrast as a call to political action, with the doctrine of the priesthood of all believers as the most effective weapon for tearing down the now famous "three walls" protecting papal authority.

Chapter four contains my exploration of the social and political context of papal claims related to temporal authority. I will consider the development of the doctrine of papal authority as it related to secular and temporal authority from the Middle Ages to the early modern period. Such an examination is critical in order to understand more fully the issues with which Luther was dealing when he wrote "To the Christian Nobility of the German Nation."

The focus of chapter five will be an examination of the text "To the Christian Nobility of the German Nation" in light of the political context in which it was written. Whatever the reasons behind Luther's decision to write his now famous address to the Christian nobility, it is clear from the text that Luther was aware of the history of doctrine that was utilized by the church to enforce adherence to papal authority in secular matters, especially in such documents as the "Donation of Constantine" and *Unam Sanctam*. Additionally, he was aware of, and in fact utilized, an already formulated set of protests which had become a rallying cry for the German people against the abuses of the pope as they were to be found in the traditions of the *gravamina*. What remains to be explored is how each of these factors was either attacked or utilized by Luther in "To the Christian Nobility of the German Nation." In the sixth and final chapter I will present my conclusions and consider a trajectory for future studies.

ized. The task of the modern historian is to look past

1

Historiographical Assumptions

In *Silencing the Past: Power and the Production of History*, Michel-Rolph Trouillot points out the obvious flaw in the production of historical narratives. Though his initial observation is not in the least bit unique to him, his conclusions are worth considering, especially in light of this study.

Trouillot begins his work by making an obvious observation: humans participate in history as actors and narrators. In the vernacular, history is the story of actors and narrators. Actors participate in the sociohistorical process by doing something. Narrators serve to tell the story of what happened.[1] This view of history serves to create a dichotomy between those who make a story happen and those who tell the story. Such a view of history too easily separates the two participants in the historical process. The task of the modern historian is to look past the dichotomy of the vernacular understanding of history.[2]

A theory of the historical narrative must acknowledge both the distinction and the overlap between process and narrative. The events as they happened must finally be told but the process from event to narrative can be troublesome because it is extremely complicated. As one reviewer wrote "The practice of history necessarily generates an ambiguous twilight between reality and text, between the doers and sayers of deeds."[3]

Agents, or those who are the participants in an historical event participate in one form or another in an historical act or movement. Agents occupy positions within the historical process. Yet these agents

---

1. Trouillot, *Silencing the Past*, 2.
2. Ibid., 4.
3. Paquette, review of *Silencing the Past*, 189.

eventually become subjects who are studied by historians who seek to determine who they were and what they did by placing them into a wider context. Thus, a person who is involved in a strike becomes a striker. They have been defined and described.[4] Oftentimes the description of the person or event is based on research which does not provide the entire reality of the agent or subject. The narrator must determine what facts to report and what facts to leave out of the narrative. Does it matter that the striker is also a mother? Does it matter if the striker, who is also a mother, is incapacitated during a violent repression of the strike and is thus unable to care for her children? The determination of how to describe the striker is based upon the narrator who is all-powerful in his or her decision-making process. The narrator has full control because the narrator controls what is mentioned and what is omitted.

Yet people are not always subjects constantly confronting history. The capacity upon which they become subjects is part of their condition. This reality makes people fully historical. It engages them simultaneously in the socio-historical process and in narrative constructions of that process. Embracing this ambiguity is the first step in understanding how history works. It is the first move any student of history must make in order to fully comprehend the production of history.

With that task accomplished the student of history must then make the second move—the methodological move—and focus on the actual process of the production of history.[5] It is this second move that will inform the methodology utilized in this study.

The search for the nature of history has led us to deny ambiguity and either demarcate precisely the line between historical process and historical knowledge or to conflate the historical process and the historical narrative. For Trouillot, the process of history should not serve to answer the question, 'What is history?' Rather the historian must confront the question, 'How does history work?' What history *is* changes. How history *works* reveals processes and conditions of production of historical narratives.[6]

The production of narratives begins long before historians reach the scene. In the process of developing the historical narrative someone always enters the scene and sets a cycle of silences, or more specifically, someone decides what not to say about a particular event or series of

---

4. Trouillot, *Silencing the Past*, 23.
5. Ibid., 24.
6. Ibid., 25.

events. Silences enter the process of historical production at four crucial moments.

First, there is the moment of fact production. Someone must create the source and say something about the event or person. The person who creates the source may well be the person involved directly in an historical event. However, the source may also be the account of those present, and, at times, the source is created by someone who did not witness the event. Therefore it is important to understand something about the source in order to identify possible filters in the final narration of the person or event.

After the fact is produced it must then be assembled. Someone must decide to preserve the event through a narrative or by preserving artifacts. In this way an archive of the event is produced. Again, the decisions concerning what to retain and what to abandon as a representative of the facts also present the historian with a challenge. Who decides what to retain and what to discard? Why was the particular decision concerning the production of the archive made? What was at stake politically, philosophically, or personally for the person who collected the facts?

Eventually someone must undertake the task of creating a narrative of the person or event. This is the moment of fact retrieval. Again, this is a moment in the process where silences can easily enter the narrative. What facts will be reported and what relevant facts will be omitted? What is the rationale for the inclusion of some aspects of an event and the omission of other aspects of the event? Certainly historians must be allowed to distill information in order to create manageable narratives. Yet it must be acknowledged that a portion of the event is often untold.

Finally, according to Trouillot, there is the moment of retrospective significance. Someone must accumulate the data, examine the narratives, and complete the process by considering the significance of the event or person. This is the final moment in the creation of history. Silences can enter the narrative in this stage as well. Determining what is significant about an event or individual involves a process of discernment. What is relevant? What is compelling? What is provable? What is acceptable? All these questions present opportunities for scholars to create a narrative that suits the needs of the narrator (not to mention potential readers!) as much as it serves the process of telling the story.[7]

---

7. Ibid., 26.

Absences and silences are created in a process that is neither natural nor neutral. One engages in the practice of silencing. Mentions and silences are thus active, dialectical counterparts of which history is the synthesis. Silences are inherent in history because any single event enters history with some of its constituent parts missing. Something is always left out while something else is recorded. Thus whatever becomes fact does so with its own inborn absences, specific to its production.[8]

Trouillot outlines this process in his retelling of the story of the slave revolt on the island of Haiti. The facts of a vibrant rebellion on the part of African slaves against white owners were silenced, according to Trouillot, because historians had no way of dealing with such a narrative.[9] The story was simply not told and as a result a silence emerged in the story of slavery in the West. The prevalent story of helpless Africans enslaved by more powerful whites would have been directly challenged by the story of the Haitian rebellion. The fact that the story was not told is, to Trouillot, an example of how silences in history serve to maintain traditional understandings of power and the systems these understandings create.

Trouillot's work can also be applied to a different end in the examination of Luther's life as it has been told by modern biographers. Silences are created when aspects of Luther's life, aspects which directly impact the development of his theology, are ignored or dismissed or misrepresented. In addition, by accepting long-held assumptions about Luther's life, a silence is created due to the assumption that the whole story has been told.

This book will provide a single example which can serve as a case study of this tendency in Luther studies. In modern biographies of Luther the reality of the political dimensions of Luther's doctrines (in this case, the doctrine of the universal priesthood) are simply ignored during the moments of fact retrieval and retrospective significance. This silence serves to further a caricature of Luther as a person interested only in the soul without reference to the world. By reexamining the context in which Luther developed his doctrines, a different narrative emerges which gives voice to the silence that has existed for so long.

What remains to be discovered once these silences are acknowledged is how they influence Luther studies. A political understanding

8. Ibid., 48–49.
9. Ibid., 82.

of Luther's doctrine of the universal priesthood opens the door for new understandings of how Luther's doctrines impact the lives of those who have attached themselves to his teachings.

The method I will utilize to discern the presences of the silences in Luther studies which impact the modern understanding of Luther's universal priesthood will be to analyze the work of those who have taken upon themselves the task of writing biographies of Luther. The task of chronicling a prominent person's life story is certainly difficult, and no scholar should be accused of a lack of professionalism simply because that person is unable—by nature of the task—to tell the whole story. Yet, in examining these works a pattern emerges. This pattern has become historical fact. However, by presenting the same story and utilizing the same facts available to those who have examined the life, thought and legacy of Luther, yet recreating the narrative by concentrating on the dialectical interplay between mentions and silences, another conception of Luther will emerge.

If Trouillot's methods can be applied to Luther studies, and if the application of his methods provides a new understanding of the political Luther, then new conclusions can be made about how to define Luther's political thought. Luther is often characterized as politically conservative. This understanding of Luther can be somewhat problematic in twenty-first century North America because the notion of what makes a person conservative is tied to issues that would not have been part of Luther's understanding of the world. Thus we must understand the concept of conservative in its most basic form. A conservative is one who wishes to retain the established order. In Luther's case, he is labeled a conservative because the narrative portrays him as wishing to reform the church without calling for change in the temporal order of society.

With the help of Trouillot's method, this study seeks to challenge that notion of Luther. This study will show that Luther's desire to radically change the structures of both church and state has been silenced. A new picture of Luther emerges. Utilizing the work done by Cornell West and armed with this new narrative, one can come to the conclusion that Luther was in actuality a political revolutionary.

In his book *Prophesy Deliverance!*, West provides insightful and contemporary definitions of such problematic terms as "political," "prophetic," "revolutionary," and "Christian." West, a thoroughly modern thinker, wrote his book in order to "put forward a prophetic interpretation of the Christian tradition rooted in the Afro-American struggle against white supremacy, informed by progressive Marxist theory and fallibilistic pragmatic thought and tempered by a profound tragic sense of life..."[10]

One would be justified in asking how a twentieth-century work rooted in African-American Marxist thought can provide a legitimate lens through which to understand Luther. Certainly it would not be appropriate to simply utilize West's language in a conversation about Luther and force a connection between these two very different thinkers. However, one can utilize West's definitions in creative ways to force a new conversation concerning how one might define Luther's political thought. In addition, by reconsidering the silenced aspects of Luther's understanding of the universal priesthood, through the lens of West's definitions, a new and interesting conception of Luther and his thought emerges which can revitalize the twenty-first century understanding of a sixteenth-century doctrine.

The term "political" is defined by West as an "attempt to enrich and enable the struggle for freedom."[11] Any attempt at setting people free from structures that reduce the potential of freedom is a political struggle. Even if one were to conclude that Luther was interested only in the matters of the spirit, the fact that his was a struggle for liberation of the Christian from the bonds of the papacy could be understood as a political act. After a thorough study of the context of Luther's articulation of the universal priesthood, one must conclude that his understanding of Christian freedom had ramifications that reached far beyond Rome and influenced the notion of spiritual and temporal authority in ways that are felt even in the modern era. For this reason, the struggle for freedom in which Luther was engaged moved well beyond the spiritual realm.

West defines "prophecy" as the identification of concrete evils. "To prophesy is not to predict an outcome but rather to identify concrete evils. To prophesy deliverance is not to call for some otherworldly paradise but rather to generate enough faith, hope, and love to sustain the human possibility for more freedom..."[12] I am not suggesting that Luther would have personally espoused all the claims made by West concerning the definition of prophesy. Luther, unlike West, was happy

---

10. West, *Prophesy Deliverance*, 5.
11. Ibid.
12. Ibid., 6.

to contemplate an otherworldly paradise. Yet those who study Luther should recognize in his universal priesthood a direct attack on what he considered to be a concrete evil: the Roman understanding of the priesthood and its power rooted in the papacy. His call for all Christians to consider themselves priests and inheritors of God's power to forgive in Jesus Christ freed the individual Christian from obedience to the ordained priesthood as it was understood in the sixteenth century. He utilized no weapons other than scripture and tradition to make his claim and had no illusion that his perspective would achieve any worldly acceptance. This final point leads us to consider West's definition of a revolutionary.

West believes that the task of a revolutionary thinker is "to transform abstract talk about God and suffering into concrete enactments of existential and political struggles with no human guarantee for ultimate victory."[13] Luther's call for the political authorities to discipline the pope and understand themselves as priests capable of reforming the church was a concrete act of defiance. Yet Luther held no illusions that his plan for reform would be received by those in authority. Assuming the role of the court jester Luther informs his friend Nicholas von Amsdorf, "Perhaps I owe my God and the world another work of folly. I intend to pay my debt honestly. And if I succeed, I shall for the time being become a court jester. And if I fail, I still have one advantage—no one need buy me a cap or put scissors to my head."[14] In the final paragraphs of his treatise he remarks, "I know full well that I have been very outspoken. I have made many suggestions that will be considered impractical. I have attacked many things too severely."[15] Luther recognized that there would be no great rush to enact his reforms. In fact, he acknowledges that they might be received negatively. Yet he is nonetheless moved to disseminate his ideas in the hope that they may indeed find some support among the civil authorities.

Finally, in a case study such as this West's definition of the concept of the "Christian" could fuel an interesting discussion concerning the type of Christian Luther was. West defines the term "Christian" in the context of his definitions of politics, prophecy, and revolution. In order to turn the concepts into meaningful descriptors of types of ac-

---

13. Ibid., 6.
14. LW 44:123.
15. LW 44: 216-217.

tions, he attaches them to an agent, the Christian person who confronts "the darker sides, and the human plights, of societies and souls with the weak armor of compassion and justice."[16] A Christian is a political person when he or she seeks to enrich and enable the struggle for freedom, not simply temporal freedom, but the freedom to live in dignity and peace. A Christian is a prophet when he or she works to identify concrete evils in the world. A Christian is a revolutionary when he or she transforms theology into concrete acts of engagement with evil. Equipped only with compassion and justice (presumably rooted in the person of Christ, though West is less than adamant about this particular point), informed by what West calls "my Marxist heritage," he goes on to proclaim the political, prophetic, and revolutionary Christian lives in the hope of new life lived in "revolutionary patience in the face of an ice age that aborts any immediate chance for fundamental social change."[17]

After giving voice to the many silenced aspects of Luther's articulation of the universal priesthood, one could easily attach West's definitions to Luther. Understanding Luther in light of these facts which inform the definitions scholars use to describe Luther as a political person should lead to a renewed and vigorous discussion as to how twenty-first century thinkers classify Luther in terms of his understanding of the relationship between faith and the structures of the temporal world.

I hope to add a new voice to Luther studies where there has remained a great silence. Luther's universal priesthood is, in part, a political doctrine that constitutes a revolutionary strain in Luther's thinking that can only be described as radical. Luther's political understanding of the universal priesthood is a challenge to the concrete structures of his day which were built upon a cosmological foundation that came under attack as a result of the Protestant Reformation. Luther undertook the work of exposing and destroying this structure with no expectation that his attack would ever deal a serious blow to the institutions of his day. In this way he takes his place among other thinkers who acted in accordance with revolutionary principles, as defined by Cornel West.

In order to make these claims we must first identify the silences. We will accomplish this task in our next chapter.

---

16. West, *Prophesy Deliverance*, 6.
17. Ibid., 8.

2

Biographical Appraisals of the Political Dimensions of Luther's Universal Priesthood

For the sake of this case study it is important to determine how biographers have understood Luther's influence on the political landscape of sixteenth-century Germany. As Martin Brecht has noted in his extensive biography of Luther, "Finally, the biographical task furnishes important orientation and criteria for Luther research, which is sometimes problematically fixed one-sidedly on the history of theology."[1] For the sake of this study I have chosen those works which are generally familiar to students of the Reformation in Germany.

The scope of this study does not allow for an in depth examination of how each author has characterized the impact of Luther as a political thinker throughout the course of his long life. Thus an overview of each author's attention to Luther's 1520 treatise "To the Christian Nobility of the German Nation Concerning the Betterment of the Christian Estate" will be presented.

The question to be asked of each work is simple. In light of their appraisal of Luther's "To the Christian Nobility of the German Nation," does the biographer acknowledge any connection between Luther's evangelical doctrine of the universal priesthood and the temporal and secular reforms that Luther presented in the treatise? More to the point, does the biographer suggest in any way that Luther's theology was linked to his understanding of the temporal realm of existence? If the answer is "no," we have discovered a silence in the story of the development of the doctrine of the universal priesthood.

In the final analysis, the answers to these questions will be as varied as the authors who have undertaken the monumental task of writing

---

1. Brecht, *Road to Reformation*, xi.

about a man like Luther and his theology. Based on the time the text was written, the political context of the author, and the intended audience of the book, one should expect different approaches to Luther's thinking. It is precisely because these studies represent such different contexts that the conclusions of this study will be of importance.

We should first be clear about how medieval thinkers understood concepts like church and the temporal realm.[2] In the medieval context of the western world, the notion of Christendom, or a Christian commonwealth, was taken for granted. As we will examine in more detail below, this Christendom was a manifestation of the mystical body of Christ with mystical patterns that composed the details of the mystical body.[3]

Within this Christian commonwealth there existed two forces, the *ecclesia* and the *respublica*. Each force was instituted by God and given a role within the mystical body. The *ecclesia*, or church, possessed the power to bind and loose, the *potestas clavium*. The *respublica*, or the temporal power, was the visible agent to whom God had given the power of the sword so that evil might be kept in check. It possessed the *potestas gladii*. The pope was the head of the church. Temporal leaders were the head of the temporal state. In this worldview the state played a negative role. Its task was to hold back the power of evil.[4] However, as we will discover in chapter four, the medieval conception of the *ecclesia* concluded that any power, or sword, possessed by the temporal authorities was essentially on loan from the pope. Thus, all temporal power was controlled, at least conceptually, by the church. With these facts in mind one can conclude that the church was, *de facto*, the primary temporal authority. This is not to say that the church's conception of authority was accepted completely by all medieval people. Yet this conception of the source of temporal authority was the church's conception and, as evidence will show, what the church believed about itself had significant influence on temporal structures in the Middle Ages.

My own biases will certainly be present in my presentation of the following biographical works. It is my presupposition that Luther was aware of the political dimensions of his articulation of evangelical the-

---

2. The medieval conception of temporal and spiritual authority will be dealt with in detail in chapter 4.

3. Schwiebert, "The Medieval Pattern," 100.

4. Ibid.

ology, as evidenced in his pamphlet "To the Christian Nobility of the German Nation" and his development of the doctrine of the universal priesthood as articulated in that document. In addition, beyond being aware of the political dimensions of his thought, I will argue that he intended his theology to change the structures of his world, ecclesiastical and temporal, impacting the office of the keys and the temporal sword. I undertake such a program of study in order to build upon it in future works which will focus particular attention on the political dimensions of Luther's theological writings.

Roland Bainton, *Here I Stand*

Roland Bainton has written one of the most influential and widely read biographies of Martin Luther. Though intended for a popular audience, Bainton should also be credited with writing a thorough examination of Luther's life, theology, and legacy that remains helpful even for scholars.

Bainton begins his assessment of Luther's "To the Christian Nobility of the German Nation" by recalling that Luther had tried unsuccessfully to appeal to the pope for the needed reform of the church. Characterized as the next logical step, Bainton focuses on the text through which Luther called upon the political authorities of his day. He asserts that by referring to the nobility Luther was actually calling upon the entire ruling class in Germany from the emperor on down.[5]

Bainton characterized Luther's position in the treatise by claiming "no one in a thousand years had so championed the civil state as he."[6] Luther's reinterpretation of baptism as a "sociological sacrament" which empowered all Christians to proclaim the gospel implied that in a Christian society, "Church and state are mutually responsible for the support and correction of each other."[7] However, according to Bainton, Luther was in actuality more concerned with the purification of the church than the development of a new understanding of the secular order.

Although Bainton was willing to place Luther at the head of all those who may have championed the idea of the civil state, he concludes

5. Bainton, *Here I Stand*, 152.
6. Ibid.
7. Ibid.

that Luther's whole attitude toward the reformatory role of the magistrate is essentially medieval. What made it different was its theological tone and the religious premise upon which it was built.[8]

In the final analysis, Luther was, according to Bainton, a conservative. He was a builder, not a destroyer who wished for the traditional Christian ethic to remain intact.[9]

Yet, Bainton pays close attention to the ways that Luther understood the orders of creation and how that ordering impacts the Christian in society. For Luther the gospel could be lived out only in the midst of secular callings, yet he refused to call them secular. As he had extended the priesthood of all believers, so likewise he extended the concept of divine calling, vocation, to all worthy occupations. God calls people to labor because God labors.[10]

In order to make his point Luther recognized three areas of human society and relationships that were instituted by God: ecclesiastical, political, and domestic.[11] Bainton is quick to conclude that Luther was finally only concerned with the ecclesiastical realm, comfortable to leave the state to civil magistrates.[12]

Any impact that Luther had on the political realm was purely incidental. According to Bainton, Luther was not interested in politics, but he could not avoid them.[13] If Luther was ever really interested in articulating ideas that would impact the understanding of the civil state they were limited to his articulation of the so-called doctrine of two kingdoms.[14]

Martin Brecht, *Martin Luther: His Road to Reformation 1483–1521*

Martin Brecht's three volume biography of Luther is one of the most extensive examinations of Luther's life to find its way into print in the English language. His aim in writing such a biography "with one pen" is

8. Ibid., 154.
9. Ibid., 232.
10. Ibid., 233.
11. Ibid., 235.
12. Ibid., 236.
13. Ibid., 238.
14. Ibid., 241.

to help unify the recent trends which had begun to include in the traditional theological examination of Luther's life such methodologies as socioeconomic studies of Luther's background, psychological studies, the influence of late medieval theology on Luther's reformation, and the political dimensions of Luther's thought. For this reason it is no surprise that of all the biographies examined in this study, Brecht presents the most comprehensive examination of Luther's address to the Christian nobility.

Setting "To the Christian Nobility of the German Nation" apart from Luther's previous writings, Brecht notes that in his address to the German nobility Luther does not present an exposition of scripture but rather "a proposal and warning to the German nobility."[15] In Brecht's opinion the treatise was not directed towards the political authorities, "which would have been more precise and would also have included the cities,"[16] but to the Holy Roman Emperor, Charles V, and members of the German nobility.[17]

Brecht, like many others, points to the reality that Luther's reform proposals were not entirely unique. They were built upon the protests that had been presented to the pope in the form of the *gravamina* at the Diet of Augsburg in 1518, adopting "the demands of the *gravamina* movement, making himself its spokesman."[18] Yet Brecht is quick to point out, somewhat too hastily it seems, that Luther was not particularly influenced by the *gravamina*. Rather, he claims that Luther had come to his positions concerning the proper program of reform independently.

In order to place theological teeth into the mouth of popular protest against the political power of the Roman Curia, Luther developed his doctrine of the priesthood of all believers as articulated in "To the Christian Nobility of the German Nation."[19] Yet Brecht is consistent with many other Luther scholars in adding a quick caveat: Luther was not so much interested in making a political statement with his universal priesthood. Instead, Luther came to articulate his understanding

---

15. Brecht, *Road to Reformation*, 369.

16. Ibid.

17. In this regard he is at odds with Bainton who assumed that the address was written for all the political leaders in Germany from the emperor on down. See Bainton, *Here I Stand*, 152.

18. Brecht, *Road to Reformation*, 371.

19. Ibid.

of the priesthood of all believers as part of an overall theological and exegetical program rising from the doctrine of justification.[20] Indeed, Brecht makes the bold declaration that Luther never in his life thought to question the existing secular order.[21] Though Luther was "concerned about energetically decentralizing the church, combined with strongly reducing Rome's central authority,"[22] there is no hint in Brecht's work that Luther made any of these decisions with the hopes of fundamentally changing the political realities of the secular world in Germany. This is perhaps due in part to Brecht's attention to the fact that Luther was unwilling to attack those old and accepted practices of the church which helped care for noble families.[23] In this way Brecht provides some rationale for why Luther was silent on some forms of social and political realities. In the final analysis, Brecht characterizes Luther as a conservative. His program was a reform program and was not to be understood as a call for the destruction of previously existing institutions in order to replace them with something new.[24]

Taken as part of a whole, Brecht understands the writing of Luther's treatise to the Christian nobility as a continuation of the work he had begun in 1519, namely, writings which had already begun to sketch out a plan for the reform of piety and church life. Brecht is quick to add that the unique quality of "To the Christian Nobility of the German Nation," as stated earlier, was that it marked a point in Luther's life and writing in which he was able to "transform his new theological understanding into a comprehensive program . . ."[25]

James Kittelson, *Luther the Reformer*

In the preface of his work on Martin Luther, Kittleson reveals the purpose behind the writing of his book. He intends to provide a work on Luther which has as its target audience the nonspecialist reader. Kittleson's work serves as an attempt to describe the personality of Luther and the context that revealed his personality. Not much is written

20. Ibid., 372.
21. Ibid., 371–72.
22. Ibid., 373.
23. Ibid., 374.
24. Ibid., 375.
25. Ibid.

about Luther's political thought; rather he concentrates on how politics impacted Luther's life and vice versa. Kittleson suggests that though Roland Bainton has already written such a volume, a new work taking into account new discoveries and methodologies would be a welcome addition to the lay reader.[26] In particular, he hopes to bring together studies which reveal Luther's connection to economic, social, religious, political, and theological structures of his day.[27]

By 1519, and into 1520, Luther began to apply himself to addressing issues related to the "practicalities of the Christian life."[28] He began by applying his new understanding of the faith to the practices of the church, in particular the sacraments. Luther was becoming more and more convinced that the primary issue at stake in the life of the church was the "promises of God that called forth trust in his goodwill. In this way he denied the church any power over the life of the individual Christian."[29]

Kittleson asserts that by the time he had written "To the Christian Nobility of the German Nation," the break between Luther and Rome had already been politically irreparable.[30] The only option for resolution would have been either for Luther to recant or for the pope to repent. Neither would come to pass. Almost as if to make this breach final and permanent Luther wrote his now famous treatises of 1520.

Kittleson remarks that in the modern era Luther's "To the Christian Nobility of the German Nation" is remembered because of its theological content rather than for the practical impact the document had in the sixteenth century.[31] However, as Kittleson points out, there can be no doubt that the treatise was a call for political reform. Luther used "To the Christian Nobility of the German Nation" as a tool for recruiting supporters for his cause. By writing the work in German and calling upon the strong anti-Roman sentiments in Germany, Luther had written a strongly political document.[32] As a consequence

---

26. Kittleson, *Luther the Reformer*, 14.
27. Ibid., 17.
28. Ibid., 146.
29. Ibid., 149.
30. Ibid., 150.
31. Ibid., 151.
32. Ibid., 151–52.

of his writings both Luther and the reform movement had become a political fact of life.[33]

Kittleson, along with one other author who will be explored below, comes close to acknowledging the full extent to which Luther's "To the Christian Nobility of the German Nation" was a political document. However, he stops short of providing a detailed analysis of the political context of Luther's treatise and certainly makes no attempt to connect the theological concept of the universal priesthood and the call for reform in the temporal realm.

Bernard Lohse, *Martin Luther* and *Martin Luther's Theology*

Bernhard Lohse's book, *Martin Luther: An Introduction to His Life and Work*, is part biography, part overview of Luther's theology. By creating an interplay between Luther's life story and Luther's theology, Lohse effectively lays the foundation for an examination of the variety of issues about which Luther wrote and preached.

Throughout the book Lohse takes seriously the impact that Luther had on the political realities of his day and beyond. After exploring the historical, cultural and political context in which Luther lived and wrote, Lohse begins to exegete Luther's writings.

Of particular importance to this study are Lohse's comments concerning the interplay between theology and politics in Luther's writings. Lohse rightly acknowledges "the theological and ecclesiological controversies of the time were inseparably involved in the conflicts of interest among politicians, the estates, and economic groups" and that Luther himself played a central role in the conflicts that arose in Germany after 1517.[34]

Lohse consistently presents Luther as a conservative who sought to maintain the political order of his day as it applied to the temporal authorities. His overall impression of Luther is that he did not intend for any reforms to be implemented without the cooperation of the duly appointed authorities,[35] thus explaining Luther's response to the

---

33. Ibid., 220.
34. Lohse, *Introduction*, 40.
35. Ibid., 51.

peasants' uprising.[36] As for the church, Luther had no need to consider the restructuring of the church with his doctrine of the universal priesthood.[37]

Throughout his work on Luther, Lohse maintains that Luther's primary contribution to the conversation concerning the relationship between church and state was his treatise "Temporal Authority."[38] Other treatises, such as "To the Christian Nobility of the German Nation" are presented as part of Luther's overall understanding of the office of ministry.

Lohse makes this point abundantly clear when he observes that the primary importance of Luther's treatise to the nobility is to be found in its theological claims, not the social reforms he laid out in the treatise.[39] Lohse thinks that it is necessary to separate the theological portion of the text from the political reforms. In this way, he rejects the possibility that one served the other and that both the theological and political dimensions of the document served as a unified whole. This claim would seem to be inconsistent with Lohse's statement that to separate theology from social and political motivations is "clear evidence of a misunderstanding of the nature of religion."[40]

In *Martin Luther's Theology: Its Historical and Systematic Development*, Lohse treats the subject of the universal priesthood under the rubric of office and ordination. Lohse comes close to the point when he claims "statements about the universal priesthood always serve to counter the resistance of the Catholic hierarchy and especially the papacy to demands for reform."[41] However, Luther did not simply speak of the "independence" of temporal authority from the influence of church hierarchy, as Lohse suggests. Rather, for the sake of reformation, he subjected the church to the temporal realm and called on the temporal arm of power to exert influence and control over the church by enact-

36. Ibid., 55, 58.
37. Ibid., 184.
38. Ibid., 52–53, 186ff.
39. Ibid., 127.
40. Ibid., 40.
41. Ibid., 290. Lohse also makes a rather problematic claim that "At no time did he [Luther] draw consequences for congregations from his doctrine" (291). This point can be directly challenged by examining Luther's treatise "Concerning the Ministry" where he literally spells out how the universal priesthood should direct Bohemian congregations in their choosing and installing preachers for their congregations.

ing ecclesiastical reforms and overseeing the ordination of ministers (e.g., the church in Bohemia). Lohse seems to miss the point when he asserts "when Luther spoke most pointedly of the universal priesthood, he always held to the particular task of the ministerial office."[42] If by "ministry" Lohse means any form of service he may be correct; however, Lohse himself asserts that Luther used the term "minister" to describe the work of a pastor.[43] But what of the way that Luther spoke most pointedly of the tasks of temporal authority under the rubric of the universal priesthood?

Certainly Luther's understanding of the priesthood of all believers was rooted in his overall theological agenda. Lohse is correct when he locates the priesthood of all believers in the larger conversation about the office of ministry and the communion of saints. Yet a silence emerges from the unqualified identification of the universal priesthood as a purely ecclesial concept without reference to the multiple dimensions of the doctrine. By ignoring the political dimensions of the universal priesthood, Lohse has given credence to all those who would claim that Luther's reforms were not intended to reshape the political world of his day (and the equally troubling assumption that Lutherans ought not seek to reshape today's political world at all). This common assumption limits the boundaries of Luther research. It limits Luther's contribution to the world of politics to an amorphous idea about two-kingdoms and creates a misconception that Luther was simply a theologian whose ideas were co-opted by princes and electors, a point will be discussed in more detail below.

A close study of the universal priesthood reveals a picture of Martin Luther as politically aware and willing to shape the relations between church and state with his articulation of theology. In particular, the treatises "To the Christian Nobility of the German Nation" and "Concerning the Ministry" reveal Luther's assumption that a proper understanding of the universal priesthood would certainly have significant political consequences as a result of the undermining of the temporal authority of the pope.

---

42. Ibid., 291.
43. Ibid., 290; see also 293ff.

Richard Marius, *Martin Luther*

Richard Marius' biography of Luther, *Luther: The Christian between God and Death*, appears at first glance to be nothing more than an attempt to present anew work already done by others. Marius seems to have adopted some of the very same premises that were made manifest in Erik Erickson's psycho-biography of Luther.

As if the potential lack of originality is not enough, Marius also begins his work with a rather subjective, if not downright hyper-biased, statement that "Luther represents a catastrophe in the history of Western civilization."[44] Throughout the book the same theme reappears: the world would have been better off without Martin Luther.

Marius' work revolves around the theme that many of Luther's own struggles, and by extension the struggles of the Reformation, were rooted in his lack of faith in the existence of God and God's ability to raise people from the dead.[45] This is a problematic assertion based on some interesting examinations of Luther's writings and a consideration of the context in which Luther lived. This assertion clearly colors Marius' understanding of Luther as a political figure, as we shall see. When the reader considers all of these themes the reader is tempted to believe that there is nothing of real value in Marius' work besides some well-written prose.

Throughout the book, Marius hopes to answer the unanswerable question that has occupied many biographers before him: why did Luther think and act the way that he did? His answers seem to revolve around his assumption that Luther was swept away in a series of events that began with his uncertainty about his own death and salvation.[46] Yet one possibility remained absent from Marius' work. Never did he assume that Luther was a learned man who was committed to changing the structures of his day so that they would fit his understanding of the kingdoms of the world and the kingdom of God. In the end, Marius appeals to the modern audience by focusing on Luther's psychology and largely dismisses Luther's ability to think politically. Indeed, the "political" Luther is largely ignored until the rather predictable chapter deal-

---

44. Marius, *Martin Luther*, XII.
45. Ibid., XIII.
46. Ibid., XII, 419, 428.

ing with Luther's 1520 treatises. From there Marius deals briefly with Luther and the princes and finally the peasants' war.

In his review of Luther's "To the Christian Nobility of the German Nation," Marius concludes that Luther had written a largely unrealistic treatise based on impossible assumptions about the ways of princes. His analysis of the treatise: Luther was ignorant in matters political because he had no real experience with princes and political leaders. Furthermore, any conception of princes and the nobility that Luther may have possessed arose from an ideal image of princes as a result of his isolation in an Augustinian cloister. After the writing of his political treatise in 1520, Marius concludes, he lost his "illusions."[47]

Even in the midst of his assertions about Luther's ignorance in matters political, Marius acknowledges Luther's attempt to join his arguments to the traditions of the *gravamina*.[48] Nevertheless, Marius understood Luther's concluding remarks in "To the Christian Nobility of the German Nation" as an acknowledgment that his ideas were hopelessly unrealistic and provided proof positive that Luther himself saw his own ideas as impossible.[49]

As far as Marius was concerned, "Luther had no interest in leading a secular reformation of society. A man preoccupied with the horror of death, avid to believe in a Christ holding the key to resurrection and the life everlasting, was not made of social revolutionary stuff."[50] Herein lies the influence of Marius' thesis on the question of Luther as a political figure. Luther was simply too caught up in his own faith struggles to care about worldly matters. Applying this logic to questions of contemporary social justice issues Marius boldly proclaims, "…it is difficult to find anything in Luther favoring practical organization of the abused to gain a better earthly life for themselves…Christ existed not to give us a better life here but to offer hope against the certainty of death."[51]

In the final analysis, on the issue of the political dimensions of Luther's thought Marius offers the same tired caricature of Luther as a monk swept into a whirlwind because of some inner theological struggle. This image of Luther lacks an acknowledgment that Luther,

47. Ibid., 240.
48. Ibid., 242, 396.
49. Ibid., 244.
50. Ibid., 419.
51. Ibid., 427–28.

as a thinker and leader, was aware of what was happening around him. Indeed, this assertion assumes that Luther was unaware and therefore uninvolved in the political life of his day.

Heiko Oberman, *Luther*

Heiko Oberman's classic biography of Luther provides a wealth of information for anyone who wants to study the social and political dimensions of Luther's thought, life, and times. An examination of Luther's life does not begin in detail until the third chapter of the book. Oberman spends a number of pages laying out the social, religious, and political climate of Luther's time and in so doing reveals to the reader his own commitment to understanding Luther in the context of his reactions to and influences on the political workings of his world.

All this is done with great attention to the reality that Luther was, above all, a Christian whose reaction to the structures of his day was a result of his religious commitments. Luther, in the eyes of Oberman, was clearly a political figure. In his discussion of "To the Christian Nobility of the German Nation," Oberman is quick to point out that the work was not simply an exposition of his new theology, but was also a manifesto and a political pamphlet.[52]

He is also cautious not to overstate Luther's political aims. To those who saw the transformation of society as a preparation for the messiah Luther "disappointed them, for his reformation did not seek to transform society in order to prepare the way for the millennium."[53] Rather Luther sought a transformed society rooted in faith, which would address abuses in order to improve the world, not ready it for the coming Christ.[54]

Oberman is consistent throughout his book on this point. Luther was a political figure, fundamentally concerned with earthly realities. In his exposition on "To the Christian Nobility of the German Nation" he describes the document as a political pamphlet and warns the reader that the "national-patriotic features of Luther's thinking should not be obscured."[55] His treatise to the emperor and temporal authorities

52. Oberman, *Luther*, 41.
53. Ibid., 61.
54. Ibid., 72.
55. Ibid., 41.

marked a new moment in Luther's life and work as it was an appeal to the general public, not colleagues or church leaders.

Luther's primary theological concern, according to Oberman, was that scripture was being subordinated to papal authority. This reality signaled the presence of the anti-Christ in the Holy See and was a sign of the last days.[56]

Oberman makes the claim that the primary concern of the document as a whole is not the theological portions of the text; not the articulation of the universal priesthood and its usefulness in tearing down the "walls" protecting papal authority. Instead, Oberman believes that the primary issue at stake in the document is the presentation of the national program of reform.[57]

What remains interesting about this claim is that Oberman, perhaps inadvertently, manages to separate the theological dimensions of the treatise from the program of reform. Oberman recognizes the theological implications of the reform program. The program of reform provides the basis for national repentance.[58] However, he does separate the doctrine of the universal priesthood from the "primary concern" of the document. This would certainly suggest the possibility that the call for reform could be made independently of the new articulation of evangelical doctrine.

Oberman finally concludes that Luther probably did not expect for his reforms to be taken seriously. Luther, however, was not overly concerned with the practical aspects of his thought. Luther was only concerned with what was necessary.[59] Luther held no assumptions that there would be a golden age until the return of Christ.[60] His task was to call for action because the action was right and holy, not because it was practical.

E. G. Schwiebert, *Luther and His Times*

Though Schwiebert's work ranks as the oldest of the volumes examined in this study, his examination of Luther's life and the treatise ad-

56. Ibid., 43.
57. Ibid., 45.
58. Ibid., 47.
59. Ibid., 46.
60. Ibid., 47.

dressed to the Christian nobility remains relevant and informative. Though aware of and interested in modern critical methodologies in the field of historiography, Schwiebert nonetheless represents a school of Luther biographers who bring to the task a significantly "Lutheran" bias. His remarks in the opening lines of his book, ". . . no one can really understand Martin Luther but a Lutheran . . ." betray his own convictions. Yet a glimpse of his professionalism can be seen in his next remark, ". . . but perhaps no Lutheran can maintain a purely academic approach towards Luther."[61]

Schwiebert was quite comfortable speaking of Luther's influence and impact beyond the realm of theology. From the opening paragraphs of his work he acknowledged the role Luther played in shaping political affairs by making quick allusions to Luther's "To the Christian Nobility of the German Nation," which Schwiebert claimed served to prove that Luther had become "the voice of the Saxon court."[62]

Schwiebert places his discussion of "To the Christian Nobility of the German Nation" firmly within the context of Luther's struggles with the sacramental system of the Roman church, especially the traditional understanding of penance.[63] Additionally Schwiebert understood the period between 1517 and 1520 as a time when Luther's understanding of religion had developed into "something entirely spiritual, a personal relationship with God. Faith in God became the chief factor in a person's relationship with God and the church."[64] Thus, with a new understanding of the church emerging, it was inevitable that a new conception of society would follow. Such a conception was made manifest in "To the Christian Nobility of the German Nation." Building upon a foundation laid by 1519 at the Leipzig Debate and in his treatise on the mass, Luther began to attack the papacy and questioned whether or not it was of divine origin. By 1520 Luther had begun an all out frontal attack on the papacy and his new vision of the church.

Before discussing the content of "To the Christian Nobility of the German Nation" Schwiebert presents an overview of the prevailing opinions (up to 1950) concerning the historical circumstances which lay behind the penning of the treatise. He concluded that a variety of

61. Schwiebert, *Luther and His Times*, 1.
62. Ibid., 5.
63. Ibid., 445.
64. Ibid., 454.

influences are discernable in this particular "brochure," all of which indicate that the political realities of his day had certainly influenced Luther's decision to write and publish "To the Christian Nobility of the German Nation."

According to Schwiebert the unique effect of the treatise was Luther's call for escape from "the 'tyranny and wickedness of Rome,'"[65] a teaching that was made manifest in the doctrine of the priesthood of all believers. The result of such a position was to create the principle by which territorial princes were given the right to influence and bring about religious reforms in their lands.

With the removal of the distinction between layperson and clergy, Schwiebert argued, the functions of the state were automatically widened.[66] He was also quick to note that Luther had not created these realities all on his own. Certainly there were traditions of protest and assertions of state autonomy from the papal curia that predated Luther. Luther provided the theological basis for such claims and as a result, "The influences of this tract on the German nobility is difficult to overemphasize..."[67]

Some Conclusions

All but one author included in this study made the claim that when articulating the doctrine of the priesthood of all believers in "To the Christian Nobility of the German Nation" Luther was primarily interested in the reform of the church and its understanding of the office of ministry. This argument would be sufficient if it were applied to "The Babylonian Captivity of the Church," or "The Freedom of a Christian," as we will see in the next chapter of this study. Yet this assertion lacks the proper understanding of the doctrine as it was presented in "To the Christian Nobility of the German Nation." Though several authors (Bainton, Oberman, Kittelson, and Schwiebert) acknowledge that Luther was interested in the political realities of his day, Schwiebert alone insists that the priesthood of all believers was part of Luther's reform program for the secular realm. While other authors share Schwiebert's view, they exist outside the mainstream voices which serve to set the boundaries

---

65. Ibid., 468.
66. Ibid., 470.
67. Ibid., 473.

of discussion concerning Luther's life and thought. Bainton, Kittelson, and Oberman see only accidental connections between the universal priesthood and the reforms of secular society that Luther advocated.

Brecht, Lohse, and Marius completely dismiss or perhaps ignore the possibility that the universal priesthood was used by Luther to provide a new vision of both the church and the temporal powers. Perhaps this is a consequence of the conclusion, despite Lohse's warning, that theology and politics can be separated. Regardless of whether this consequence was intended by the authors, it stands as the result of their work.

Lohse concludes that the important part of "To the Christian Nobility of the German Nation" is to be found in the theological portions of the text, not the program for reform of the secular powers.[68] What is implied is that the theological foundation of the texts can be separated from Luther's advocacy in the treatise for secular and ecclesial reforms. Luther never suggests that he was writing two separate treatises published under the same name. On the contrary, Luther builds his program of reform on the foundation of his doctrine of the universal priesthood. Indeed, if it were not for the theological foundation Luther would have provided nothing unique in his reformation program. Others had called for the exact same changes. Luther added a theological dimension to already existing grievances. Though Lohse certainly comprehends the political implications of Luther's thought one is left to wonder if he fully understand the source of Luther's political thought.

Brecht makes the bold assertion that never in his life was Luther interested in making changes in the secular realms of life. One could justify making the exact opposite claim: that throughout his life Luther was constantly interested in changing the secular structures of his day.

If we were to make such a claim it is possible for us to prove it from Luther's works. Luther was quite willing to apply his theology to the issues of war, poverty, agriculture, regressive taxation, and education among other things. Luther constantly addressed political figures and institutions such as the Senate in Prague, his own elector, princes, nobility, and the emperor himself.

---

68. Oberman makes the same error, but with different emphasis when he claims that the heart of the treatise is to be found in the program for reform, not the "three walls."

The conclusion of my research—that modern biographers do not take into account the political dimensions of Luther's universal priesthood—could be nuanced by including the work of other authors who are off the radar of many students of the Reformation. Authors such as Walter Altmann and Gerhard Brendler do deal with the political dimensions of Luther's doctrine of the universal priesthood. However these authors are outside the mainstream and approach the issue of Luther's life and work from an overtly political position.

Walter Altmann, *Luther and Liberation*

One glaring exception to the underlying assumptions of my thesis is found in the book *Luther and Liberation: A Latin American Perspective*. Altmann approaches Luther from the standpoint of a Latin American theologian who, due to his particular context, allows for no uncommitted distance when it comes to considering the doctrines espoused by Luther.

In his articulation of Luther's universal priesthood, Altmann makes the following observation, "The discovery of the 'royal priesthood of all baptized believers' implied militant support for transformation of the church and of the political reality."[69] If I were to offer a word of criticism to this remark it would be that Altmann does not speak strongly enough. By laying out a specific plan of action based on his evangelical theology, his call for militant transformation was hardly "implied"; it was explicit.

Altmann is right on the mark when he points out that for Luther "Christians who held office could dedicate themselves—as 'justified priests'—to tasks in the political, economic, and social arenas."[70] Yet he hesitates at this point in the book to make the corollary statement: Christians who held political office could dedicate themselves—as "justified priests"—to tasks in the ecclesiastical arenas. This is perhaps owing to Altmann's justifiable concern that the church could become a puppet of the state.

However he chooses to interpret the intent of Luther's doctrine, Altmann understood that "Luther derived Christians' political voca-

---

69. Altmann, *Liberation*, 4.
70. Ibid., 9.

tion from their 'royal priesthood.'"[71] The impact of this new vision was that the papal monopoly over the interpretation of scripture would be broken.

In commenting on Luther's "To the Christian Nobility of the German Nation," he points out that taking into account the audience of the document helps understand Luther's motivations.

> In addressing himself to the Christian nobility, Luther insists that their political function does not emerge autonomously and arbitrarily but from their universal priesthood as baptized Christians. As Christians called to political office, therefore, they ought to carry out the necessary economic, political, and social reforms of the German nation.[72]

The point to Altmann's interpretation of the universal priesthood seems to be a reiteration of the responsibilities of the government towards the people. It is an understandable call to the political powers to remember the poor and the oppressed. Yet as I have hinted at above, Altmann does ignore the reality that Luther was interested in more than the repentant commitment to the oppressed on the part of the princes. Luther's political thought was much more multidimensional than that. Luther was seeking an end to papal hegemony over more than just the right to interpret scripture.

Altmann misses the point—or perhaps ignores it!—that Luther intended that the princes actually intervene in the life and workings of the church. Certainly this reality could be frightening to anyone living in the modern world. Yet this is exactly what Luther demands of the princes. Thus even Altmann, despite acknowledging the universal priesthood's political dimensions, refuses to articulate its implications beyond the realm of ministry. Certainly he sees it as a doctrine that calls for a lay-led ministry of advocacy, but he misses the deeper significance of the role Luther envisioned for the princes in the life of the church itself.

Gerhard Brendler, *Martin Luther*

Gerhard Brendler wrote his assessment of the life and legacy of Martin Luther while a citizen of the German Democratic Republic. He in-

---

71. Ibid., 47.
72. Ibid., 70.

tended his work to be a reminder that the purpose of the DDR was to build socialism in a baptized country.[73] Thus Brendler's biases are immediately recognizable. For Brendler, Luther was a revolutionary, the father of the first revolution in German history. "Theology, reformation, and the confrontation with revolution stamped his life so markedly that they stand at the center of this biography."[74]

Brendler has no problem linking Luther's theological and social thought. His assessment of Luther acknowledged that "The more Luther linked his theological goals with daily concrete problems, the more he became the foreman of the new reformed consciousness."[75] For Brendler, it was precisely Luther's willingness to encounter the world that helped him to formulate the principles of the reformation, including the concept of the priesthood of all believers.

This understanding of Luther's life and legacy is understandable when one considers Brendler's reason for writing his biography. His intention was to try and find a way to move beyond the typical Marxist critique of Luther as a person who sided with the status quo against a revolutionary uprising of the peasants. Instead, Brendler was trying to strengthen the claim that Luther laid the foundations for future revolutions by laying waste the medieval systems of domination and power. "Seen from this perspective, the hammer-blows in Wittenberg in October 1517 posting the ninety-five theses that initiated the Reformation, were echoed exactly four centuries later in October 1917..."[76]

In his assessment of "To the Christian Nobility of the German Nation," the author restates a rather well-accepted formula that Luther "was not consciously concerned with the transformation of social and political conditions but rather with the freedom for preaching the gospel."[77] He further states that Luther's relationship to the masses was built on the assumption that for Luther, "The masses were...a raw material to be shaped rather than a base upon which to build politically."[78] On this point, the reader can recognize glimpses of a comparison between Luther and Lenin. Luther, like Lenin, sought to change the structures of

73. Brendler, *Theology and Revolution*, 1.
74. Ibid.
75. Ibid., 164.
76. Ibid., 14.
77. Ibid., 174.
78. Ibid..

his society by "reeducation" of the masses but did not rely on them to be the source of or directors of that change. Because of this understanding of Luther and the masses, Brendler posits that it was only natural for Luther to turn his attention to the nobles, kings, and princes of German lands to provide the power behind his movement.

He intended that those in positions of power destroy the ranks of stratification within the church. Only accidentally did these notions of equality eventually find a place in the secular arena. "With his fundamental principle of the priesthood of all believers, Luther also provided a frame of reference for those social forces that were not at all willing to be satisfied by ecclesiastical reform alone."[79]

Another consequence of Luther's address was the development of a German nationalism. This factor, among others, helped to transform Luther's theology into a specifically German ideology.[80]

The limitations of the effectiveness of Luther's demands for reform could be forgiven. After all, the "absence of organization and official communal institutions" limited the ways in which reforms could be carried out in the secular arena, such as the call to end begging by mendicant orders. Yet the importance was to be found in the fact that his theology was beginning to function as an ideology. Through his understanding and application of the doctrine of justification the "ideological function of Lutheran theology was developed on the plane of the relationship of the individual to society."[81]

Summary

Why are the political dimensions of the universal priesthood missed by so many mainstream biographers? Some possible explanations can be identified by understanding the underlying assumptions found in the methodologies of those who undertake Luther studies.

To begin, because of the influence of traditional Marxist thought on many scholars, political reformation and revolution is understood only insofar as it leads to radical systemic change (a point that is called into question by progressive Marxists like West). Indeed, Luther's suggestions for political reform were largely ignored. For this reason it could

79. Ibid., 177.
80. Ibid., 179.
81. Ibid., 182.

be said that Luther's political reforms essentially failed. Additionally, the reforms that Luther called for have been interpreted as essentially conservative and sometimes reactionary. There are many reasons for this interpretation of Luther, not the least of which is the hijacking of Luther by German nationalists in the nineteenth century. Thus the political Luther is relegated to a few caricatures and stereotypes (lackey of the princes, uninterested in the "world" because he was preoccupied with issues related to salvation).

Furthermore, there is a willingness to overstate assumptions made about why Luther was engaged in developing, or rediscovering, an evangelical theology. Authors such as Marius assume that Luther was motivated by a rather simple preoccupation with his own spiritual struggles. This approach to Luther assumes that scholars have insights into Luther's psychological condition and the depths of his faith struggles.

What is needed is a new method, a method that can help find ways of speaking about politics and theology using the evidence at hand. In addition, a new understanding of reformation and revolution must be considered. In this case study, using the methods already presented in chapter one, we will attempt to apply this method to Luther by exploring the context and content of "To the Christian Nobility of the German Nation." By considering the historical issues challenged by Luther and the historical context of the document, we will be better able to understand what Luther actually says in his treatise and make more tenable conclusions about how Luther understood the interplay between theology and politics.

Before this works is done we must first ask and answer the question of how Luther utilized the doctrine of the universal priesthood throughout his career. Such a study will help students of Luther to see just how unique and exciting Luther's articulation of the universal priesthood was in his 1520 treatise "To the Christian Nobility of the German Nation."

A Consideration of Luther's Body of Work on the Topic of the Universal Priesthood

BEFORE AN EXAMINATION OF THE POLITICAL AND TEMPORAL DIMENsions of the universal priesthood—as it was articulated in "To the Christian Nobility of the German Nation"—can be undertaken it is appropriate to first examine how Luther understood the universal priesthood throughout his career as a reformer. A study of a variety of texts is needed in order to place "To the Christian Nobility of the German Nation" in its proper theological and historical context. Such an examination will reveal that Luther did not write about the universal priesthood exclusively in terms related to the politics of his day. Indeed, Luther often wrote of the doctrine within the context of simple ecclesiastical and sacramental reforms. Thus, much of what is assumed about Luther's understanding of the universal priesthood by biographers and theologians alike does apply to most of what Luther wrote on the subject. In fact, "To the Christian Nobility of the German Nation," when studied alongside Luther's other writing on the universal priesthood, stands in stark contrast as a call to political action—with the doctrine of the priesthood of all believers as the most effective weapon for tearing down the now famous "three walls" protecting papal authority.

Romans 3:20 (1515–1516)

There is no doubt that as Luther was writing his commentary on Romans 3:20 in the winter of 1515–1516, he held to the traditional Roman understanding of the priesthood, with no hint of the leveling effect that his doctrine of the universal priesthood would come to have in the years to follow.

In the third chapter of Paul's letter to the Romans he makes the claim: "For 'no human being will be justified in his sight' by deeds prescribed by the law, for through the law comes the knowledge of sin." One can imagine what Luther would do with this verse in 1520, yet in 1515 his words seem to give us a glimpse into his doctrine of justification,

> The works of the Law are those, he says, which take place outside of faith and grace and are done at the urging of the Law, which either forces obedience through fear or allures us through the promise of temporal blessings. But the works of faith, he says, are those which are done out of the spirit of liberty and solely for the love of God. And the latter cannot be accomplished except by those who have been justified by faith, to which justification the works of the Law add nothing, indeed, they strongly hinder it, since they do not permit a man to see himself as unrighteous and in need of justification.[1]

Yet in his application of the doctrine of justification he made no attempt to reconsider the traditional understanding of the priesthood. Luther gives the following example to make his point:

> Here is an example. If a layman should perform all the outward functions of a priest, celebrating Mass, confirming, absolving, administering the sacraments, dedicating altars, churches, vestments, vessels, etc., it is certain that these actions in all respects would be similar to those of a true priest, in fact, they might be performed more reverently and properly than the real ones. But because he has not been consecrated and ordained and sanctified, he performs nothing at all, but is only playing church and deceiving himself and his followers.[2]

He states further that it is not in the performance of functions that one becomes a priest. The priesthood rests on the authority of the sacrament of ordination as Luther made clear when he wrote that the priest merely plays church without the sacrament of ordination.[3] Obviously this perspective changes by the time he wrote "To the Christian Nobility of the German Nation."

---

1. LW 25:234.
2. LW 25:235.
3. LW 25:235.

"A Treatise on the New Testament, that is, the Holy Mass" (1520)

The year 1520 marked a turning point in the life of Luther and the church. In June of that year the papal bull condemning Luther was signed, and the breach between Luther and Rome was nearly complete. Luther attacked "papal absolutism" in his major treatises of 1520, creating a position of opposition against the pope and his authority that was adopted by many Germans. The writings of 1520 were not the works of a "humble monk seeking enlightenment on doctrinal matters but that of a bold leader of the people demanding a revolutionary break with Rome."[4]

Published in July 1520, Luther's "Treatise on the New Testament" is widely considered to be his first attempt at articulating his understanding of the priesthood of all believers. At the heart of the work is Luther's attack on the doctrine of the mass as sacrifice. The New Testament that Luther here addressed is the testament that was made by Christ at the last supper; the fundamental part of the mass.

Luther's primary concern was that the mass had come to be seen as a sacrifice, not a testament. For Luther there could be no sacrament without a testament because the words of promise were more important than the signs attached to the promise. Thus he reasoned that the mass had been turned on its head because, in his view, the signs had replaced the promises of God. Luther meant to set it aright in this treatise. "What the mass is intended to do, we take upon ourselves to do; and what we ought to be doing, we turn over to the mass to do. All this is the work of unlearned and false preachers."[5]

Luther believed that the sacrifice of the mass is not a sacrifice that is offered to God directly, but to Christ who mediates on behalf of all sinners. "in this way it is permissible, yes profitable, to call the mass a sacrifice; not on its own account, but because we offer ourselves as a sacrifice along with Christ."[6] All Christians are priests when they offer themselves to God and receive God's testament and sign of the promise. It is faith which believes the testament, receives the sign and offers the believer to God. This is the true priestly office. Thus, all believers

---

4. Grimm, *Reformation Era*, 109.
5. LW 35:99.
6. LW 35:99.

are spiritual priests before God through faith in Christ.[7] "Therefore all Christian men are priests, all women priestesses, be they young or old, master or servant, mistress or maid, learned or unlearned."[8]

For Luther, the consequence of this new understanding of the mass was that any understanding of the mass that relied on sacrifice without the testament, sacrament and faith of the believer was rejected. Thus masses for the dead were no longer appropriate. Certainly one should pray for a loved one, Luther reckoned, because through faith all things are possible. But to suggest that the sacrament could be done on behalf of another person removes the role that the faith of the believer plays in the sacrament and reception of the testament.

Despite the obvious individual freedom that the new doctrine suggested, a handing over of the authority of the gospel to all believers, Luther did not envision individual priests/believers doing individual masses "in open fields." He was adamant that people must come together in order to strengthen each other's faith because "the outward seeing and receiving of the sacrament and testament" will "move each other to the increase of this faith." Christians hold mass "outwardly" because of their need for the word of God and the strength given through the preached word and the outward signs.[9]

People of God in Christ are able to offer the sacrifice of the mass because they are able at all times to offer themselves to God through faith. In this way Luther redefines the term mass, but does not call for the wholesale abolition of the sacramental rituals. Luther still envisioned that people would come together and celebrate the mass in common.

In this treatise we see no hint of the ecclesiastical leveling that is so often associated with the doctrine of the priesthood of all believers. Luther was not calling for an end to church hierarchy; rather he was calling for a better understanding of the relationship between God and humanity as it is mediated by Christ.

"The Babylonian Captivity of the Church" (1520)

In "The Babylonian Captivity of the Church" one encounters Luther in the process of a headlong attack on the Roman sacramental system. The

7. LW 35:100.
8. LW 35:101.
9. LW 35:104–5.

importance of this entire treatise, and the extensive content, makes it impossible to do justice to the document in a few pages.

Luther was certain that he was not offering any innovations when it came to his sacramental theology. Rather, he understood himself to be returning to the roots of Christian belief in regards to the sacraments. "It was not the church which ordained these things, but the tyrants of the churches, without the consent of the church, which is the people of God."[10]

In "The Babylonian Captivity of the Church" Luther defines a sacrament and by extension rejects all but three of the sacraments practiced by the Roman church: baptism, penance and Holy Communion. In so doing, he longs to speak of only one sacrament, Christ himself, with three sacramental signs.

We find Luther's explanation of the universal priesthood in his exposition on the "sacrament" of ordination, as one would expect. Luther begins by attempting to convince the reader that Roman ordination is not about ministry, but rather it is about holding onto power through a false sacrament. The consequence of this understanding of the sacrament is division within the church and what he understands to be a devaluation of baptism.

> They have sought by this means to set up a seed bed of implacable discord, by which clergy and laymen should be separated from each other farther than heaven from earth, to the incredible injury of the grace of baptism and to the confusion of our fellowship in the gospel. Here, indeed, are the roots of that detestable tyranny of the clergy over the laity. Trusting in the external anointing by which their hands are consecrated, in the tonsure and in vestments, they not only exalt themselves above the rest of the lay Christians, who are only anointed with the Holy Spirit, but regard them almost as dogs and unworthy to be included with themselves in the church.[11]

Clearly Luther acknowledges the need for leaders in the church. However, the work done by those who had been set aside by priests was to be the work of ministry given to one priest by the many for the sake of the congregation, "If they were forced to grant that all of us that have been baptized are equally priests, as indeed we are, and that only the

---

10. LW 36:23.
11. LW 36:112.

ministry was committed to them, yet with our common consent, they would then know that they have no right to rule over us except insofar as we freely concede it.[12]

He then goes on to specify exactly what sort of work is to be done by these minister priests:

> From this it follows that whoever does not preach the Word, though he was called by the church to do this very thing, is no priest at all, and that the sacrament of ordination can be nothing else than a certain rite by which the church chooses its preachers.[13]
>
> Therefore my advice is: Begone, all of you that would live in safety; flee, young men, and do not enter upon this holy estate, unless you are determined to preach the gospel, and can believe that you are made not one whit better than the laity through this "sacrament" of ordination![14]

"The Freedom of a Christian" (1520)

Of all Luther's writings on the evangelical faith, perhaps none is more familiar to the average student of Luther than "The Freedom of a Christian." Though most people are aware of the "95 Theses," chances are those who have decided to commit time to reading Luther began with this treatise.

"The Freedom of a Christian" is one of the great evangelical treatises of 1520, written by Luther in a conciliatory spirit. Published in November 1520, the treatise contains an overview of Luther's evangelical theology with a focus on how that theology will impact the daily life of the believer. It was hoped that this text could stem the tide of fury heading toward Luther. The text was written for Pope Leo X in hopes of assuring the pontiff that Luther's criticisms were not directed at him personally. However, the pope—if he ever read the document—would have surely been unimpressed with the tone and content. Luther wrote to Leo as an equal and even dared provide him advice. Nowhere in the text is there the slightest hint that Luther was ready to retract any of

---

12. LW 36:112.
13. LW 36:113.
14. LW 36:114.

his teachings.[15] Indeed, with his notion of the universal priesthood, Luther continues his attack on papal claims to absolute authority over the church.

Within this treatise the most famous of all of Luther's axioms can be found:

> A Christian is a perfectly free lord of all, subject to none.
> A Christian is a perfectly dutiful servant of all, subject to all.[16]

These words encapsulate Luther's understanding of a justified and sanctified Christian, thus setting the tone for Christian theology and ethics. Yet it is also a concise explication of Luther's doctrine of the priesthood of all believers, as Luther himself explains.

In the process of laying out his evangelical theology, Luther explains that the inheritance of Christ, which he gives to all Christians in a happy exchange (a metaphorical marriage between Christ and the baptized), is the twofold honor of priesthood and kingship. This is in keeping with the traditions of the Old Testament in regards to the inheritance of the firstborn son.[17]

> Now just as Christ by his birthright obtained these two prerogatives, so he imparts them to and shares them with everyone who believes in him according to the law of the above-mentioned marriage, according to which the wife owns whatever belongs to the husband. Hence all of us who believe in Christ are priests and kings in Christ, as I Pet. 2[:9] says; "You are a chosen race, God's own people, a royal priesthood, a priestly kingdom, that you may declare the wonderful deeds of him who called you out of darkness into his marvelous light."[18]

In this respect, every Christian is a king, lord of all things as an inheritance from Christ himself. This is not to suggest that there is to be no temporal authority. On the contrary, in the spiritual realm faith rules in the midst of enemies and "is powerful in the midst of oppression." Because faith has set the believer free, the believer needs nothing outside this faith in order to exercise Christian liberty.[19]

---

15. LW 31:329-30.
16. LW 31:344.
17. LW 31:353.
18. LW 31:354.
19. LW 31:355.

Not only is the believer a free king, but he or she is also a priest forever. He or she is able to intercede for others before God and teach the faith. In this way, believers are servants for one another as Christ served humanity on the cross and in the resurrection.

This universal priesthood/servanthood of all believers, coupled with the universal kingship, does not do violence to the difference between people and the offices they hold in the world and in the church. "Although we are all equally priests, we cannot all publicly minister and teach."[20]

Answer to the Hyperchristian, Hyperspiritual, and Hyperlearned Book by Goat Emser in Leipzig— Including Some Thoughts Regarding His Companion, the Fool Murner (1521) (With reference to "Dr. Luther's Retraction of the Error Forced upon Him by the Most Highly Learned Priest of God, Sir Jerome Emser, Vicar in Meissen, 1522")

Luther's relationship with Jerome Emser was passionate and complicated. Emser, whom Luther took to calling "goat" because of the presence of a goat on Emser's coat of arms, began his relationship with Luther by inviting the reformer to a banquet at his home. The now legendary meal took place in July of 1518 following a sermon Luther preached at the Castle Church in Dresden.

A year later Emser "defended" Luther's positions as orthodox by making the claim that Luther did not support the positions held by Jon Huss. He drew these conclusions from his hearing of Luther's positions at the Leipzig Debate. Luther recognized this "defense" as a trap that would force him to recant his positions that were in agreement with Huss.

Luther and Emser would come to blows following the publication of Luther's "To the Christian Nobility of the German Nation." Emser had concluded that Luther, especially in his understanding of the universal priesthood, had not taken seriously the spirit of scripture but rather followed the letter. Emser concluded that although all Christians share a spiritual priesthood, there remained a consecrated priesthood which

20. LW 31:356.

could not be so easily applied to the entire body of Christ. Luther reacted in two phases by maintaining the distinction between estate and office that he had written about in 1520, and later by accusing Emser of being afraid of the loss of power and the right to tyranny that the evangelical doctrine of the universal priesthood had brought to light.

As previously mentioned, Emser attacked Luther's understanding of the universal priesthood by claiming that Luther comprehended only the letter of 1 Peter 2:9 but missed the spirit. He claimed that Luther's understanding of the priesthood of all believers necessarily led to the conclusion that all Christians were to be understood as consecrated priests. Luther rejected Emser's division of the spiritual priesthood and the consecrated priesthood by making the claim that St. Peter's words have a simple meaning that encompassed spirit and letter.[21]

Luther contended that despite Emser's assurances, Peter never once spoke of a consecrated priesthood and that Emser was mistaken if he believed Luther had spoken of a consecrated priesthood. According to Luther, the New Testament spoke only of the spiritual priesthood.[22]

What had come to be understood as priestly functions were never called priestly in scripture but were rather called "ministry, servitude, episcopate, and presbytery." Luther explained that the term priest came from words like *presbyteros* in Greek and *senior* in Latin and *eldest* in German, all of which indicated age, not status, and that any meanings the term priest had come to possess came about because no word of scripture had retained true meaning.[23]

In his argumentation, Luther attacked the priestly estate not the office of ministry, and maintained that the external differences between Christian priests applied to office, not estate. If there was to be any discussion about what is "consecrated," it would have to be in the context of office and left out of any discussion of estate. It was not Scripture, but rather the pope's law, that made distinctions between the people and rulers. The term priest had come to be applied to the likes of bishops who serve as temporal lords. In this way they derived from the higher spiritual estate, a sense of their right to exercise political authority

---

21. LW 39:152.
22. LW 39:153.
23. LW 39:154–55.

which Luther had concluded was the right of those who held temporal offices.[24]

Luther spoke in more detail about the political implications of this new understanding of the priesthood in his final tract against Emser, "Dr. Luther's Retraction." He accused Emser and the papists of fearing their loss of power. Luther caricatured Emser and the papists by placing the following statement on their lips: "If we lose the priesthood all our power is lost." He continued, "For the power associated with the priesthood, namely, preaching, celebrating mass, dispensing the sacraments and using the keys is well known."[25] He concluded, "They should be subject to the common assembly as servants and should discard their tyranny."[26]

Defense and Explanation of All the Articles (1521)

In 1520 Pope Leo X issued the now famous bull *Exurge Domine*, which threatened Luther with excommunication because of forty-one of Luther's theological propositions, which Rome declared heretical. Luther responded in two ways. He famously burned a copy of the papal bull in December 1520. He also responded as any good theologian would, by writing his responses to each of the forty-one articles condemned by the pope. This process began in November 1520. Eventually Luther defended himself in four works, two in Latin and two in German.

In defense of the thirteenth article, Luther maintained that the pope had no special authority that was not already given to the most humble of priests. He once again maintained that "it is not the work of the priest but the faith of the penitent which effects the forgiveness of sins."[27] In this instance Luther was addressing specifically the sacrament of penance, yet his understanding of the universal priesthood, though not specifically mentioned, provided much of the foundation for his argument against papal authority.

Luther maintained that the sacraments are the common property of all Christians arguing that "all baptisms and all masses are equally valid, wherever and by whomever they are administered . . . Everything

24. LW 39:157–60.
25. LW 39:229–30.
26. LW 39:238.
27. LW 32:50.

depends on the faith of him who receives it, not on the holiness, learning, rank or power of him who administers it."[28]

Once again it must be said that the doctrine of the universal priesthood is not here being articulated in its fullness. Yet one sees the impact of this theology. The power to forgive, which is the common property of all Christians, is effective only when grasped by the faith of the believer. Thus the role of the priest, especially the primary priest in Rome, is put in its proper place.

"The Misuse of the Mass" (1521)

The treatise "The Misuse of the Mass" is, for all intents and purposes, a footnote to Luther's most important treatise on the subject of the Roman mass, "The Babylonian Captivity of the Church." Luther had come to recognize that no significant changes would be made in the church's understanding of the sacramental system and sought to present a more detailed and radical understanding of how the mass should be transformed to reflect evangelical theology.[29]

The treatise is split into three separate units, of which the first has specific relevance to this study. In part one of the text, Luther deals with the nature and the role of the priesthood as it applies to the understanding of the sacrament of communion. Here Luther distinguishes between the spiritual priesthood and the outward priesthood, and assaults his opponents on three fronts.

His first attack is against the outward priesthood in favor of a spiritual priesthood. "Every true Christian really ought to know that in the New Testament there is no outward, visible priest, except those whom the devil has exalted and set up through human lies. We have only one single priest, Christ, who has sacrificed himself for us and all of us with him."[30] If a priesthood exists it exists only as an inheritance from Christ himself. "This is a spiritual priesthood, held in common by all Christians, through which we are all priests with Christ. That is, we are children of Christ, the high priest; we need no priest or mediator other than Christ. "Every priest (Heb. 5[:1]) is appointed in order that

---

28. LW 32:52.
29. See introduction, LW 36:129ff.
30. LW 36:138.

he might pray for the people and preach." Thus every Christian on his own may pray in Christ and have access to God..."[31]

Because of this reality the outward priesthood is, to use Luther's language, overthrown.[32] What then, according to Luther, is the role of the shared priesthood? If as Luther asserted in "The Babylonian Captivity of the Church" the role of the priest cannot be to offer the sacrifice of Christ in the mass, which was made once and for all on the cross, what does the Christian priest offer? Here is his second assault against the Roman priesthood. According to Luther, the Christian offers the "rational sacrifice."

> ... the priestly office, which is nothing else than a rational sacrifice; not the offering of irrational cows or calves, as in the law, but the sacrificing of one's self to God. This, however, is supposed to be common to all Christians; therefore all Christians must be priests. What will you answer to this, you miserable pope?
>
> Is this not meant to refer to all Christians? Are not all Christians built like living stones on Christ, and so built upon him that they are priests who sacrifice not irrational animals, but themselves, after the example of Christ—spiritual sacrifices, when in the Spirit they put to death the deeds of the body? (Rom. 8[:13]). What will our poor miserable idols and counterfeits say to this? Does Peter here also make two kinds of sacrifice, just as the mouth of falsehood has invented two kinds of priests for him? We are all commanded to make this sacrifice, whatever kind of persons we may be; therefore the priestly office is incumbent upon all of us. Hence it is clear that we are all priests.[33]

His final front is in relation to the office of the priest. For Luther the priest is not the sole officiant over the sacrifice of Christ, but rather fills the office of preacher. This, too "like priesthood and sacrifice, is common to all Christians."[34] Luther even makes way for the possibility of women preachers—though not in a way that would please modern feminists—by declaring if no men are available, even women can be allowed to preach.[35]

31. LW 36:139.
32. LW 36:139.
33. LW 36:146.
34. LW 36:149.
35. LW 36:152.

In all these things Luther maintains a consistency with his other writings. The priesthood of Rome, because it is limited and because it is based on the sacrificial understanding of the mass, is to be rejected in favor of an evangelical priesthood shared by all, with stipulations that the office is to be carried out by competent persons for the sake of good order.[36]

Luther continues his treatise with an attack on the episcopal office because Roman bishops "shamelessly dare to call themselves princes ..."[37] Here Luther seems to keep his promise that this text, and the evangelical theology that it contains, can "change the whole spiritual and human order."[38]

Luther attacked the office of bishop because it had become a fiefdom, controlled by the pope with the intention of maintaining a hold on "the properties, bodies, and souls of all men, and treats them more harshly than any tyrant or heathen treats his possessions; and that they call feeding the sheep of Christ!"[39] It is obvious that the implementation of Luther's theology has secular consequences. Luther is aware of these consequences and advocates for them. If the bishops are simply priests among priests, who gets the land and property formerly held by the Roman church? Clearly we see here the reality that Luther seeks to change both the spiritual and secular order with his evangelical theology. What is missing is a plan of action dictating what to do if his changes are put in place.

Commentary/Sermons on 1 Peter 2:1–10 (1522–23)

In his exposition of 1 Peter 2:5, Luther once again attacked the notion that there is an external priesthood that exists in addition to the spiritual priesthood of all the baptized. "All the externals of the priesthood have now come to an end.... everything is spiritual."[40]

Luther also lifted up the happy exchange through which the believer is granted all that belongs to the Son. "Thus only those are the holy and spiritual priesthood who are true Christians and are built on

36. LW 36:149.
37. LW 36:154.
38. LW 36:133.
39. LW 36:157.
40. LW 30:52.

the Stone. For since Christ is the Groom and we are the bride, the bride has everything that the Groom has, even his own body."[41]

Luther upheld the principle that the true priest occupies an office devoted to teaching, preaching, offering spiritual sacrifices, and prayer. Indeed much of Luther's exposition on 1 Peter is reminiscent to what he had written earlier.

He once again took up the issue of the universal priesthood in his commentary on 1 Peter 2:9. Luther believed that the verse "requires no commentary; for it speaks explicitly of all those who believe."[42] In the few paragraphs devoted to this verse, Luther expressed what the term priest, rightly understood, represents. He was certain the Roman theologians would maintain the term priest. His only comment was that they may call themselves priests but that they were not to be seen as priests of God "for they cannot adduce a single word from Scripture in defense of this."[43] He would rather that the term priest be replaced with a descriptor better suited to his theology: Christian.

"That a Christian Assembly or Congregation Has the Right and Power to Judge All Teaching and to Call, Appoint, and Dismiss Teachers, Established and Proven by Scripture" (1523)

In 1522 the community of Leisnig began the process of conversion to the evangelical cause. The community needed to reorder itself and its ecclesiastical structures and called on Luther to provide help and guidance.

Luther agreed to lend his support to the endeavor and met with members of the parish in September 1522. On the table for discussion was how best to articulate the congregation's right to call a pastor, and how a common chest ought to be set up for the needs of the parish.

These issues became important to the assembly at Leisnig due to the fact that a parish pastor, Heinrich Kind, had been assigned to the church by Antoninus, abbot of Buch, a local Cistercian monastery. Kind converted to the evangelical cause and was immediately recalled by the

---

41. LW 30:53.
42. LW 30:62.
43. LW 30:62.

abbot with the support of many local townspeople and the peasantry. Some prominent members of the parish, however, wished to retain the services of Kind, and a conflict arose over who had the authority to determine who would serve as parish pastor of the church.

The abbot attempted to simply assert his traditional authority over the church, but to no avail. Eventually the abbot, perhaps sensing that more conflict in this arena would do further damage to his authority, decided against continuing his objections. The congregation asked Luther to add his name to their congregational constitution, thereby giving credence to the parish's decision to call its own pastor. Luther was also asked to provide the congregation with an evangelical liturgy to be used in the parish.[44]

In January 1523, members of the parish in Leisnig visited Luther once again and asked him to compose a document which would provide scriptural support for the changes being made in their community. Luther eventually agreed and composed a series of documents, beginning with the document now being examined in this study, which was printed in May 1523.[45] Luther also contributed a preface to the community's Fraternal Agreement on the Common Chest of the Entire Assembly at Leisnig, a document which will be examined in detail below.

In his treatise "That a Christian Assembly or Congregation has the Right and Power to Judge All Teaching and to Call, Appoint, and Dismiss Teachers, Established and Proven by Scripture," Luther begins his work by defining a congregation as the place where the gospel is preached. On this foundation, Luther takes away from the Roman church authorities the right to impose pastors on congregations because, in his estimation, "bishops, religious foundations, monasteries, and all who are associated with them have long since ceased to be Christians or Christian congregations..."[46] because of their reliance on human ordinances rather than God's word.

For Luther, Christ gives to his sheep the power to know his voice. It is for this reason that the congregation, not the institution of the church, is best able to judge teachings and choose pastors. Thus the argument is not being laid upon the foundation of the universal priesthood, but

44. LW 45:165.
45. LW 39:303.
46. LW 39:305.

on an ecclesiology that focuses on the authority of the congregation, as sheep over the shepherds. Nonetheless, Luther does eventually include the universal priesthood as he explains the need for giving some sheep the authority to lead congregations.

> ... since in these last accursed times the bishops and the false spiritual government neither are nor wish to be teachers—moreover, they want neither to provide nor to tolerate any, and God should not be tempted to send new preachers from heaven—we must act according to Scripture and call and institute from among ourselves those who are found to be qualified and whom God has enlightened with reason and endowed with gifts to do so.
>
> For no one can deny that every Christian possesses the word of God and is taught and anointed by God to be priest, as Christ says, John 6[:45], "They shall all be taught by God," and Psalm 45[:7], "God has anointed you with the oil of gladness on account of your fellows." These fellows are the Christians, Christ's brethren, who with him are consecrated priests, as Peter says too, 1 Peter 2[:9], "You are a royal priesthood so that you may declare the virtue of him who called you into his marvelous light."[47]

He ends his remarks by acknowledging that the office of preacher is the highest office a Christian can hold. He bases this claim on the fact that Jesus did not baptize, he only preached.[48] For this reason the hierarchy of the Roman church has inappropriately given power to those whose office does not require them to proclaim the word.

"Ordinance of A Common Chest: Preface to the Fraternal Agreement on the Common Chest of the Entire Assembly at Leisnig" (1523)

In his preface, Luther does not specifically mention the doctrine of the universal priesthood. Yet he says of the document: "I have seen fit to have this ordinance of yours printed, in the hope that God will so add his gracious blessing that it may become a public example to be followed by many other congregations, so that we, too, may boast of you, as St. Paul boasted of the Corinthians that their effort stirred up many

47. LW 39:309.
48. LW 39:314.

others [II Cor. 9:2]."⁴⁹ He suggests that the "governing authorities take over the property" of local monasteries and that, "In carrying out this policy the permission of pope or bishop is not to be sought beforehand, neither is their ban or anathema to be feared; for I am writing this solely for those who understand the gospel and who have the authority to take such action in their own lands, cities, and jurisdictions."⁵⁰ In this way Luther continues to advocate that the temporal authority of the church is to be completely disregarded, even as it applies to the calling of local parish pastors.

These words add weight to the ordinance itself, which expresses the reliance of the authors on the doctrines of Christian freedom and the universal priesthood to justify their actions. In regards to filling the pastoral office, the authors "exercise, and employ our Christian liberty solely in conformity with the precept and ordinance of the divine biblical Scriptures . . ."⁵¹ This statement sends a shot across the bow of any who would suggest that the congregation owes obedience to abbot or bishop.

> We, the parish assembly, by virtue of our universal priesthood, have always had and should have had the full right and authority, which we reserve wholly to ourselves and in no way relinquish, to acquire all properties and rights, hereditary lands, quitrents, and supplementary rents, proprietary rights, buildings, manor places, gardens, fields, pastures, stores, and chattels personal without exception, insofar as they were in every case granted and assigned by the original donors, and by those who later supplemented these bequests to the priestly and pastoral office here in our midst, and have in times past thereto belonged and therein been used—this was the substance of the negotiations and the decision reached between ourselves and the abbot of Buch in the chancellery of our most gracious lord, the Elector of Saxony—which properties and rights are now on deposit in our common chest.⁵²

This declaration of independence from the church authorities has both spiritual and temporal consequences. It is one thing to suggest that a congregation has the right, by means of the universal priesthood, to call

49. LW 45:169.
50. LW 45:172.
51. LW 45:177.
52. LW 45:179.

its own pastors. It is quite another to suggest that this universal priesthood gives a congregation the right to take over the care and operation of lands and property traditionally belonging to the Roman church.

"Concerning the Ministry" (1523)

The fact that Luther was not the first to challenge the authority of the pope is easily proven with a reference to the Bohemian Christians. From the time of Huss, many Bohemians had insisted on the right of the laity to receive the sacrament of communion in both kinds, and the freedom for priests to preach from the scriptures.

Despite the fact that the followers of Huss accepted the vast majority of Roman doctrine, the Pope refused to provide an archbishop, thus reducing the opportunity for local churches to receive ordained priests. This was the case from 1421–1560.

Luther was aware of the Bohemian resistance and hoped that they would continue to fight the papacy and perhaps come over to the side of the evangelicals. He was convinced by a Bohemian pastor, Gallus Cahera, that the Bohemians were ready to make the final break with Rome.

Though Luther encouraged the Bohemians to remain adamant in their opposition to Rome, they eventually came to reject Luther's understanding of the ministry described in this treatise. The insistence of Cahera that the Bohemians were fully ready to accept the Reformation was revealed to be wishful thinking on the part of an ambitious pastor.

Despite the fact that Luther's treatise bore little fruit in Bohemia, it has come to be considered one of the most important of Luther's writings on the office of ministry and the priesthood of all believers. In it, Luther rejected the priesthood in ways similar to his 1520 treatises. He also defined ministry and provided guidance on how exactly congregations should carry out new ordinations.

Luther addressed the letter to "the Illustrious Senate and People of Prague." This is in keeping with Luther's understanding that in times of emergency, it is up to temporal leaders to begin reform of the church. In his mind, it would be up to those in positions of temporal authority to enact the proper reforms in the churches in Bohemia and "break completely with Rome."[53]

53. Grimm, *Reformation Era*, 202.

He began with a warning that the letter would not endorse or reject certain rites and rituals. He made it clear that he was not concerned with the question of usages such as tonsures and anointing, though he used these images as weapons against the papacy throughout the letter. What concerned Luther was the situation in which the Bohemians found themselves. They were forced to send people to Italy to purchase papal ordination. This practice had many negative consequences, not the least of which was the problem that the priests were often not worthy of their office. In his words, "Indeed this plight of yours has given rise to a proverb, namely, that one who has earned the noose or the wheel among the Germans qualifies as priest among the Bohemians."[54]

Luther's response to this untenable situation was to advise the Senate in Prague that the people under their jurisdiction were better off to go without priests than tolerate the abuses inherent in the Bohemian church. He encouraged parents to assume the responsibilities of teaching the gospel to their children and baptizing children born in their home. He argued that Christ is present even if priests are not. Only the Word of God is necessary for the ministry. Yet this did not mean that Luther advocated a wholesale rejection of the office of ministry. His recommendations were suited to the emergency situation in Bohemia "in captivity."

Luther then moved away from speaking specifically about the Bohemian situation and expounded upon his understanding of ordination in general. In essence, even if the Bohemians could get priests ordained by the Roman church, they should not. Luther emphasized that the problem with priests ordained by bishops was that they believed that their only task was consecrating and confessing. What of the call of the parish and the ministry of the word? What of baptism? Luther held that papal priests thought of these tasks as unimportant because they did not require the indelible character of the office of ordination. Thus he concluded that they despised the word of God and replaced it with the office of sacrifice.[55]

This was at the root of all the problems that Luther identified with the priesthood as it was understood by Rome. Because the papal priests were, in his opinion, uninterested in the ministry of the Word and teaching, they served no purpose in the church. Luther upheld the arguments

54. LW 40:8.
55. LW 40:12.

he had made in his "Treatise on the New Testament," that the mass was not a sacrifice. And if the mass was not a sacrifice, then the confession that the priests demanded was not to be viewed in the traditional way. If these two propositions were true, what need did the Bohemians have of Roman priests?[56]

Throughout the treatise, Luther accused Roman priests of hiding behind these masks of falsehood. Yet he was not simply interested in uncovering lies; he firmly believed that through these deceptions (insisting on the sacrifice and the indelible character of ordination) the supposed priests of God had become "priests of Satan," trampling down Christ by insisting on the efficacy of human works and offering sacrifices daily as though forgiveness was not eternal.[57]

After reminding the Bohemians that the Pope was their natural enemy by recalling the death of Huss, Luther began to unfold his understanding of the ministry of the word and the priesthood of all believers. "A Priest is not identical with Presbyter or Minister—for one is born to be priest, one becomes a minister." [58] Through baptism into Christ all Christians share in Christ's priesthood in equal degree. Thus the functions of a priest (teaching, preaching, baptizing, consecrating the Eucharist, binding and loosing sins, praying, sacrificing, and judging doctrines and spirits) are the tasks of all Christians.[59]

The first and foremost task of a priest is to teach the Word and from this task all other priestly functions are drawn. Because this task is given to all Christians, the functions of the priest also belong to all Christians. In this way, Luther rejected the notion of a twofold priesthood; a spiritual and an external priesthood. For Luther, there was only one priesthood: the spiritual priesthood.[60]

Those who occupy a public office, what the Romans inappropriately referred to as the external priesthood, hold office for the sake of good order. They should not be called priests; but are more appropriately called ministers, deacons, bishops, stewards or presbyters. Additionally, because they serve the needs of the community on behalf of the community, the community should have the right to choose a minister from

56. LW 40:13.
57. LW 40.15.
58. LW 40:18.
59. LW 40:21.
60. LW 40:22.

within the community to serve in this office. And when the community is not being properly served, it has the right to recall a minister.[61]

Luther recognized that some in the Senate might be hesitant to make such a radical change in the calling of pastors. His response to this concern was to assure the members of the Senate that his understanding of the office of ministry was in essence the ancient custom used by the apostles and their disciples. Even so, why should the Bohemians be worried about innovation? Luther reminded them that Bohemians had been challenging the authority of the pope for many years. Was that not a novelty?[62]

After providing some practical advice about how to go about calling pastors, Luther provided some words of comfort. He assured the Senate that the princes of the world would not remain silent and would surely object to these practices in Bohemia. When their time of suffering came, they would know that God was with them.[63]

Commentary on Isaiah 66:22 (c. 1530)

Luther lectured on Isaiah from the summer of 1527 to the winter of 1530, interrupted only by a move occasioned by the plague and time in Marburg.[64] In his exposition of Isaiah 66:22, "For as the new heavens and the new earth, which I will make, shall remain before me, says the Lord; so shall your descendants and your name remain," Luther remarks that the Levitical priesthood has been shifted away from a single tribe and given to all nations.

He then moves, predictably, into his understanding of the priesthood as it should be understood among evangelical Christians. He acknowledges that, "We are all priests" and defines the priestly task as "[bringing] sacrifices to God. This he does through prayer, mediation, and worship."[65] Once again Luther stipulates that this task must not be carried out by anyone without a proper call.

---

61. LW 40:35.
62. LW 40:39.
63. LW 40:43.
64. From Heiko Oberman's introduction. LW 17:x.
65. LW 16:415.

Psalm 82:4 (1530)

Luther was inspired to write his lectures on Psalm 82 after visits to Saxon churches which caused him to consider the lack of moral and spiritual direction being provided by the churches and their leadership. By April 1530 Luther had indicated in a preface in a book on the Anabaptists, written by Justus Menius, that he had completed his book on Psalm 82. It was first published in June 1530.[66]

The tone of Luther's exposition of Psalm 82:4, "Rescue the weak and the needy; deliver them out of the hand of the wicked" is surprisingly political and temporal. In his lecture Luther is quick to point out the role of temporal authorities in church affairs. Luther reminds the hearer/reader that the princes have neglected many of their duties and have thus allowed injustice to reign in the German lands. Of these neglected duties, oversight of the church ranks high on Luther's list of concerns. "For it is the princes and lords, who ought to be advancing God's Word, who do the most to suppress, forbid and persecute it."[67] For Luther, not only should the princes and lords work to advance God's word, they should also put down opposing doctrines.

Luther gives four examples of how the princes and lords should intervene in spiritual matters. First, seditious leaders, who claim that in order to be a Christian one must abandon secular laws, should be punished "as men who are resisting temporal law and government."[68] Second, those who teach doctrines which contradict articles of faith are to be punished by secular rulers because they are "duty bound to punish blasphemers as they punish those who curse, swear, revile, abuse, defame, and slander."[69]

Third, if factions within the church create a division, both claiming the authority of scripture, and if those divisions cause endless quarreling, "let the rulers take a hand. Let them hear the case and command that party to keep silence which does not agree with scripture."[70] Note here that the authority to determine sound doctrine is in the hand of the temporal rulers, not the clergy. Fourth, in matters commonly called

---

66. LW 13:x.
67. LW 13:59.
68. LW 13:61.
69. LW 13:61.
70. LW 13:63.

adiaphora, if there is unhealthy wrangling which makes its way into the pulpits, the secular authorities are to order the offending parties to keep silent.

It is in this way that Luther introduces his comments on the universal priesthood. He makes the claim that all Christians are priests,[71] but cautions the church against letting anyone without a call speak publicly as though they occupy a pastoral office. Here he uses the examples of Carlstadt and Müntzer. The rule should be enforced that those who are not called to preach and teach be silenced.

In this way Luther places limits on the universal priesthood and seems to suggest that the temporal authorities have the last word in who should speak publicly on behalf of the church. Yet nowhere in this explanation does Luther resort to the universal priesthood as his warrant for having the secular authorities preside over spiritual questions, as he did in his treatise to the Christian nobility.

Psalm 45:11 (1532)

Luther gave his class room lectures on Psalm 45 in the year 1532 from August to November. The modern student of Luther owes a debt of gratitude to George Rörer for passing along his notes of these lectures to Veit Dietrich who prepared them for publication. Luther himself was reluctant to have them published because time constraints did not allow him the opportunity to edit and revise the manuscripts. The lectures were finally published in 1533–1534.[72]

The focus of this study is the 11th verse of Psalm 45: "and the king will desire your beauty. Since he is your lord, bow to him." In his exposition of this verse, Luther continues his thoughts on the innate monk living in the heart of all Christians, the monk who seeks inner perfection before approaching the glory of God in Christ. Luther relies on his understanding of the gift of grace, as laid out in his doctrine of justification, to combat the notion that a person can make him or herself desirous to the king, who is Christ. Only the free gift of the king makes us beautiful, as Luther indicates by saying, "internally I am beautiful by an alien adornment."[73]

71. LW 13:65.
72. LW 12:vii-viii.
73. LW 12:279.

Luther acknowledges the reality that God gives humanity a variety of gifts, but the Lord, who is to be worshipped, is more than a gift. He is the giver. "So distinguish here between the gift and the Giver. He gave the law...the righteousness of the law...miracles under the old Law ... But what are these in comparison with the fact that at last He gave Himself?"[74]

This line of reasoning leads him to comment on the universal priesthood. According to Luther "the worship of God is now the adoration of this King, not the ceremonies of Moses, the pope, monks, heathen, or Turk." Because adoration of the King is all that is necessary in worship, there is no need for distinction. "We are all priests, clothed and adorned with the same holiness of Christ, whom we receive through faith, much more beautiful than all righteousness of the Old Covenant and the papacy."[75]

Sermon on Psalm 110:4 (1535)

Throughout May and June of 1535 Luther gave a series of sermons on what he considered to be one of the most Christian psalms in the Old Testament, Psalm 110.[76] The focus of this study is Luther exposition of Psalm 110:4 "The Lord has sworn and will not change his mind, 'You are a priest forever according to the order of Melchizedek.'"

For Luther, this verse signals David's desire to elevate Jesus to the position of king, priest, and pope. In this way, he believes that "the prophet assigns both offices to Christ: He is to be the everlasting King and Priest."[77] This has some impact on how both the spiritual and temporal spheres understood by Luther to co-exist in the person of the messiah, in opposition to the dictates of Moses.

> David here contradicts Moses, in fact, the established order of God. Really, David deserves to be denounced as a heretic or a rebellious prophet and teacher for apparently presuming to grasp for the priestly office in behalf of his Descendant, in crass contradiction to God's express command. God clearly wanted the two offices, king and priest, separately maintained. This is

74. LW 12:281.
75. LW 12:289.
76. LW 13:XII.
77. LW 13:304. The same argument was made in "The Freedom of a Christain."

something which secular insight has also discerned as necessary. Yet David, according to this verse, wants to unite the kingly and priestly functions in one person![78]

This does not mean that Luther understood the kingship and priestly office of Christ as one would understand the temporal ordering of the offices of priest and king. Luther went out of his way to indicate that Christ instituted an entirely new priestly and kingly office which needed to be understood as spiritual, not temporal offices.[79] The priestly office of Christ, which he gives to the church, is to be understood far differently than the papists had understood it. This is in keeping with Luther's argument that the Roman church had given up its spiritual role in order to occupy a temporal role in the affairs in the world.

For Luther, the claim of the Roman priesthood to occupy spiritual and temporal offices to the exclusion of others was anathema. The priestly office

> consists of three parts: to teach or preach God's Word, to sacrifice, and to pray . . . If anyone does not exercise these functions of the office, but still wants to be called a priest or pope, he does not deserve this beautiful and glorious name. This applies to those who are the masks of our pope, those false bishops, along with their anointed and tonsured mob. By their entire life and conduct they bring disrepute and dishonor upon this noble name, so that it is not honored as highly as it ought to be.[80]

As he continues his exegesis, Luther contends that the Roman understanding of the priesthood assumes that Christ gave to the clergy alone what belonged to him and that the pope, by claiming exclusive control over the gifts of Christ, had usurped the power of Christ for himself alone. "Therefore, the pope argues that he alone has the priestly office and that he alone has the right and power to ordain and do what he will. Is it not a manifest lie and blasphemy to dare to teach publicly that Christ has given away or transferred His priestly office? It is as though Christ were no longer needed, as though He sat in heaven without anything at all to do, and as though He had nothing at all to do with us!"[81] This Luther could not abide.

78. LW 13:305.
79. LW 13:306.
80. LW 13:315.
81. LW 13:330.

His response was to articulate anew his understanding of the universal priesthood as a check on papal power and authority. Christ does not transfer the office of priest to an institution; rather he gives it as an inheritance to his children. "Thus we all, as I have said before, have become priest's children through baptism. Therefore it should be understood that the name 'priest' ought to be the common possession of believers just as much as the name 'Christian' or 'Child of God.'"[82]

Again Luther acknowledges that despite the fact that all are priests, only some fill the office in an official capacity as a minister, preacher, pastor, or curate. These people became priests first, then they were given their office. "Such people are to be chosen by the church only for the sake of the office. They are to be separated from the common mass of Christians in the same way as in secular government, where certain people of the citizenry or municipality are chosen and appointed as officials. One does not become a citizen by being elected burgomaster or judge, but one is elected to the office because one already possesses citizenship and is a member of the citizenry."[83] As Luther so consistently points out in other treatments of the doctrine of the priesthood of all believers, the public calling is necessary if a priest is to be chosen for an ecclesiastical office.

Sermon at the Dedication of Castle Church, Torgau (1544)

Luther was asked to preach at the dedication of the first new evangelical church to be built in Saxony. He preached on Luke 14:1-11 and used the occasion to expound on how Jesus understood the Sabbath and how Christians, in the light of Christian freedom, should enact the teachings of Jesus in Torgau and throughout the reign of God.

As he begins his sermon Luther reminds his listeners:

> My dear friends, we are now to bless and consecrate this new house to our Lord Jesus Christ. This devolves not only upon me; you, too, should take hold of the aspergillum and the censer, in order that the purpose of this new house may be such that nothing else may ever happen in it except that our dear Lord himself may speak to us through his holy Word and we respond

---

82. LW 13:330.
83. LW 13:331.

to him through prayer and praise. Therefore, in order that it may be rightly and Christianly consecrated and blessed, not like the papists' churches with their bishop's chrism and censing, but according to God's command and will, we shall begin by hearing and expounding God's Word, and then, in order that this may be done fruitfully, following his command and gracious promise, call upon him together and say the Lord's Prayer.[84]

Thus, it is not up to Luther alone to dedicate the church to the work of God. Additionally, it will not be through the rites of the church that the people of Torgau will be given a new worship space. Rather, it is the work of all the faithful to make certain that the new church building will be a place for the proclamation of the Word of God, prayer and praise.

As Luther expounds of the gospel text he makes his case by utilizing contextual analysis of the Jewish understanding of the sabbath. "It is true that at that time the particular day of the sabbath was fixed for the Jewish people, and also a specified place, a special tribe or [group of] persons, and a particular priesthood or service of worship was appointed. For all this must take place only in their country and in the temple at Jerusalem, conducted by the Levites, who belonged to the priestly tribe, from which tribe alone the ministers of the church were drawn."[85] Yet, because of the freedom given to all people in Christ, the followers of Christ

> are not thus bound to a tribe or place, so that we must adhere to one place alone and have only one race or one particular, separate kind of persons. Rather we are all priests, as is written in I Pet. 2[:9]; so that all of us should proclaim God's Word and works at every time and in every place, and persons from all ranks, races, and stations may be specially called to the ministry, if they have the grace and the understanding of the Scriptures to teach others. So we, too, are lords of the sabbath with Christ and through Christ, as he himself says in Matt. 12 [:8], "The sabbath was made for man, not man for the sabbath; so the Son of man is lord even of the sabbath" [Mark 2:27–28]. Accordingly, all those who believe in him are likewise lords of the Sabbath.[86]

---

84. LW 51:333.
85. LW 51:335.
86. LW 51:335.

In this way Luther makes his case for Christian freedom, utilizing his understanding of the doctrine of the universal priesthood.

Some Conclusions

In each of these texts Luther is dealing with a specific issue or biblical text. The common denominator in each of these texts is that Luther relies on the concept of the universal priesthood to bolster his position.

Some patterns emerge in his thought. First, the notion of the universal priesthood is commonly used as a direct attack on the authority of the pope. One can also recognize that Luther is not advocating a kind of grass-roots democracy in which there is no distinction between people or the offices they hold. Thus, the ministry of the ordained must be controlled and limited for the sake of good order. The person who serves as a minister must be a servant of all and when that person is no longer able to be a servant another is chosen to take over the office. "This is the way to distinguish between the office of preaching, or the ministry, and the general priesthood of all baptized Christians."[87]

In his early commentary on Romans 3, his understanding of the priesthood is traditional. By 1520, in his "Treatise on the New Testament" and "Babylonian Captivity of the Church" the issue at stake for Luther was the sacramental nature of Roman ordination. In these texts, along with "The Misuse of the Mass" and "Concerning the Ministry" Luther claims that ordination cannot be understood sacramentally. In "The Freedom of a Christian," Luther's universal priesthood stands as a call for a renewed commitment to Christian life. In his polemics against Emser, "Defense and Explanation of All the Articles," "Misuse of the Mass," commentary on 1 Peter, commentary on Isaiah, and commentary on Psalm 110, Luther uses the universal priesthood as a way of discussing the office of the ministry. In his work with the community of Leisnig, the universal priesthood was a sign of Christian freedom in regards to calling pastors. While exegeting Psalm 45, Luther expounded upon how the universal priesthood impacts the doctrine of justification. He also took an opportunity to take an additional shot at papal authority. In his sermon at Torgau, Luther once again used the universal priesthood as a call for renewal in Christian life and a commitment to the doctrine of Christian freedom.

---

87. LW 13:332–33.

It is also interesting to note that at times the doctrine of the universal priesthood is used as a tool for understanding—or influencing—the political realm. This is the case in "Dr. Luther's Retraction," in which Luther accuses Emser and the papists of fearing an inevitable loss of temporal power if the Roman priesthood is eliminated. In "The Misuse of the Mass," Luther is aware of the reality that the rights of bishops and priests to the properties they control would change or disappear if the priesthood is universal. In his work with the congregation at Leisnig, Luther is working directly with secular authorities in order to help the break away from the Roman church. As justification for their action, the community recalls its universal priesthood, and thus takes back its right to choose who will serve as spiritual leader in the community church. In his commentary on Psalm 82, the universal priesthood is invoked as a reminder to temporal authorities that they must control abuses in the church. Again in "Concerning the Ministry," Luther is directly dealing with the Senate in Prague and uses the universal priesthood as a justification for that community to remain rebellious in the face of the demands of the pope. In his commentary on Psalm 82, he reminds the temporal authorities of their duty to regulate the church and protect it against those who persecute it.

Knowing how Luther understood and articulated the doctrine of the priesthood of all believers is a first step towards gaining a better understanding of the political dimensions of the doctrine as it was expressed in "To the Christian Nobility of the German Nation." However, it is not until we have examined the claims of papal authority throughout the Middle Ages that we can truly comprehend the impact of the doctrine in the temporal realms.

4

The Social and Political Context of Papal Claims of Temporal Authority

According to the great medievalist, Walter Ullmann, the social ordering of Western Christian society in the medieval period constituted the cosmology upon which society was constructed.[1] The cosmos was understood as a manifestation of the Body of Christ, and, as the sole vicar of Christ, the pope could claim the right of principal authority. Temporal authority—including the authority of emperors—was understood as subordinate to papal power, especially by those who espoused the principles of papal authority. Though the conception of papal authority in the temporal realm was questioned at times, as we shall demonstrate below, the subjugation of the temporal authorities to the spiritual authorities developed gradually as the West moved from being a "neutral world" which contained two separate institutions, the church and the state to a "thoroughly Christianized world" which was, by the ninth century, encompassed by the concept of the *ecclesia*.[2] Thus, if the authority of the pope were to be challenged, the challenge would also extend to the very structures of temporal and secular power as it was understood in the medieval period.

By the ninth century there were no longer two separate institutions, the church and the temporal authority. Rather there existed two powers, temporal and spiritual, within the Body of Christ.[3] The natural world was incorporated into the spiritual world, and the result was the

---

1. Ullmann, "Boniface VIII," 58.
2. McCready, "Papal Plenitudo Potestatis," 660.
3. Ibid.

further development of the concept of papal *plenitudo potestatis*, or the plenitude of power possessed by the pope.[4]

William McCready argues that it was the Investiture Controversy that finally solidified this incorporation of the natural world into the supernatural world and justified the pope's claim that only the "functionally qualified"[5] were justified in claiming to possess authority to rule. As a result of the Investiture Controversy, it was agreed that spiritual issues must be handled by spiritual authorities. The civil powers were reduced to their secular essence, the worldly sword.[6]

By the late medieval period, it was assumed that temporal matters had no independent value and were defined only in their relation to the spiritual realm. Ullmann makes reference to the doctrine of baptism as an example of how the material world was perceived as valueless. At baptism a metamorphosis takes place where the natural person is destroyed and the spiritual person is brought into being. Thus, only those who can control this metamorphosis are functionally qualified to possess full authority.[7] Clearly this position provided only a conceptual framework for understanding the nature of the created order in the Middle Ages. The power of the priests was often challenged, yet the conceptual framework proved strong enough to weather many of the attacks that the church faced in the real world. The conflicts that arose between the papacy and secular rulers often resulted in more than just theoretical and conceptual victories for the popes.

Ullmann concludes that the peculiar imprint of western medieval society is not the division between church and state, but rather lies in the division between layperson and cleric.[8] Understanding this dynamic is crucial if one is to truly appreciate the depths of Luther's attack on the structures of his day through the articulation of the universal priest-

---

4. McCready, "Papal Plenitudo Potestatis," 661. The term *plenitudo potestatis* was originally used by the papacy to describe the power delegated to papal legates, yet by the late Middle Ages the concept was used to describe the authority of the pope in both the spiritual and temporal realms. Yet, early on, the concept of *plenitudo potestatis* indicated only temporal consequences of spiritual power. By the twelfth and thirteenth centuries the term was used by advocates of the papal hierocratic theory to speak of the ultimate authority of the pope in the temporal sphere. See ibid., 654–55.

5. Ullmann, *Growth of Papal Government*, 13–14.

6. McCready, "Papal Plenitudo Potestatis," 661.

7. Ibid., 663.

8. Ullmann, *Growth of Papal Government*, 13.

hood in 1520. Luther's universal priesthood constituted an attack on the medieval cosmology. It was this attack that made his reform proposals possible. Without the attack on the cosmology, Luther's reform proposals would have simply been a restating of the many grievances that had already been articulated in the centuries before the early modern German Reformation. By gaining an understanding of the context of the claims of papal authority in the Middle Ages inherent in medieval cosmology, we can argue more effectively the claim that the universal priesthood was an essential aspect of Luther's calls for temporal reform. Furthermore, by recognizing the role that Luther's universal priesthood played in his attack on the structures of power we can conclude that the universal priesthood constitutes a revolutionary stream in Luther's thought.

In order to place Luther's universal priesthood in its political context, we will need to explore in some detail the history sketched in the preceding paragraphs. The purpose of such an exploration is to provide the social and political context of the doctrines of papal authority in the temporal arena. First we will consider the development of the conception of papal authority, and then we will explore the various challenges made by those who wished to limit papal authority, especially in the political realm.

We will come to understand that the question of church and state was in actuality a question about cosmology in the late medieval period. Furthermore, we will discover that even though some attacked the way the pope used his power, the basic cosmology of the day remained unchallenged.

Papal and Ecclesiastical Authority in the Medieval World

It is important to note that the conception of papal authority as it related to secular authority in medieval times was much more complex than today. It is tempting to envision a distinction between church and state that simply did not exist in the medieval world. As mentioned above, the social ordering and the government of Christian society in the West during the Middle Ages constituted the cosmology upon which the entire social order rested.⁹ Medieval social life and governmental theory was based on conceptions of the body of Christ derived from the Bible, as well as the conception of the new being in Christ who resided in that body. This view of God, the world and the church was centered on a new wholeness which manifested itself in society by a strict obedience to the hierarchy found in the body of Christ on earth. Because this church was the corporate union of all believers in Christ, as St. Paul had indicated, all those who believed were governed first and foremost by the pope.[10] The main vehicle used by the papacy to promote this cosmology was canon law. "For the jurist—here it is the canonist who primarily matters—was the technician who translated the abstract cosmology into concrete terms in order to shape and define the path of society."[11]

Perhaps the most important concepts for understanding how this cosmology influenced the medieval understanding of the relationship between temporal and spiritual powers was the hierocratic theory of government and the conception of *plenitudo potestatis*. Combined with the concept of papal *principatus*, these ideas were used by the papacy to create the conceptual framework by which the pope claimed ultimate authority over both the spiritual and temporal realms. These ideas were eventually developed by canonists and shaped the cosmology of the late Middle Ages.

Early Medieval Period

Leo I, who served as pope from 440–461, understood himself as the person who functioned on behalf of St. Peter, who functioned on behalf of Christ. Thus it was he, and those who served as the Vicar of St. Peter on earth, who were best qualified to assume governmental responsibilities of Christendom.[12] We are reminded that according to Walter Ullmann, the peculiar imprint of western medieval society is not the division between church and state, rather, it lies in the division between lay and cleric as different parts of the same unit: the church.[13] Leo de-

9. Ullmann, "Boniface VIII," 58.
10. Ullmann, *Growth of Papal Government*, 2.
11. Ullmann, "Boniface VIII," 61.
12. Ullmann, *Growth of Papal Government*, 13
13. Ibid.

fined this leadership in monarchic terms. The church, under the direction of the pope, governed on the basis of *principatus*, a concept that had previously been used to describe the basis of power in the realm of government.

As Paul described the body of Christ, there were divisions between that which is spiritual and that which is of the flesh. It is this dual nature of the body of Christ that Ullmann identifies as being of fundamental importance in the medieval church: "the element ... which brings this concrete body into existence, which makes the union a corporate entity, is the spiritual element of the Christian faith: this element alone gives this body its complexion. As a body the *corpus Christi* is in need of direction and orientation ..."[14]

All are one, but there are differences in functions. In charge of this unity are the ordained priests. Given this overarching authority of the priests, what role does the emperor play in such a government? St. Ambrose had once claimed that the emperor is to be like a son, not a master of the universal church. Leo informed the emperor that his primary role was to protect the church and he made it clear to the emperor that as far as the papacy was concerned the imperial office was finite and should be understood as such. Indeed, the adjective *temporalibus* indicates a temporary state of affairs. Again, the Christian body was to be directed and governed by those who were functionally qualified, not the emperor.

In addition, the society must be directed in its actions by the divine law and teachings which are also controlled by the ordained. The emperor is not qualified to determine these laws because he is not a priest. In accordance with the principles of Gelasius I (d. 496), "It is his [Emperor's] business to learn what is the content of religion, not teach."[15] These laws, understood as divine laws, came to be codified and known as canon law.[16]

According to Gelasius, since the pope alone has the *principatus* over the Christian body, the emperor must be directed by and subordinate to the priests. In a letter sent to Emperor Anastasius, Gelasius made this claim clear. "There are in fact two, August Emperor, by whom this world is originally governed; the consecrated authority (*auctoritas*) of

---

14. Ibid., 3.
15. Davis, *First Seven Ecumenical Councils*, 211.
16. Ullmann, *Growth of Papal Government*, 447.

bishops and the royal power (*potestas*). Of these, the responsibility of the bishops is more weighty, since even for the rulers of men they will have to give account at the judgment seat of God."[17]

The secular power does not have the right to issue decrees which impact the faith because the emperor is not a priest. In short, in the Christian world the secular power has *potestas*, while *principatus* of the pope expresses itself in *auctoritas*,[18] a term which has its roots in Roman law denoting a connection to the moral and ideal spheres of life. *Potestas*, on the other hand, was simply the power to carry out temporal administrative functions. "Thus in the mind of the pope Episcopal authority is higher in some undefined degree to imperial power just as moral influence is superior to physical force."[19]

In the time of Leo I and Gelasius I the conceptions of secular and sacred existed as two parallel institutions. By the ninth century, the conceptual framework, or worldview, of the Christian world had changed. By this time "one must talk, not about two separate institutions but two powers . . . in a thoroughly Christianized world" which were made manifest in one institution, the church.[20] This was the cosmology of the medieval period in which the natural world was absorbed into the supernatural, and thus the state was absorbed into the church. For this reason, the ninth century is the locus of the root of the hierocratic theory of government which subordinated the temporal authorities to the spiritual authorities; yet it was built upon the foundation of papal *auctoritas* as it was understood since the fifth century.

The student of history realizes quickly that the rulers and emperors of the medieval world were not nearly as impotent as papal doctrine would have suggested. Byzantine emperors insisted on approving the pope before he could be duly consecrated, to name only a single example. During the thirteenth century, emperors, determined to put the papacy in check, took upon themselves the role of priest and king.[21]

The denial of monarchic power to the kings accounts for their continued resistance to the roles approved for them by the church. For Ullmann, this point characterizes the entire medieval period. "[T]he

17. Davis, *First Seven Ecumenical Councils*, 211.
18. Ullmann, *Growth of Papal Government*, 20.
19. Davis, *First Seven Ecumenical Councils*, 211.
20. McCready, "Papal Plenitudo Potestatis," 660.
21. Tavard, "Bull Unam Sanctam," 110.

hierocratic axiom of functional qualifications met with resistance on lower lay spheres" which played a role in the Renaissance call to return to ancient sources for the truth of Christian life.[22]

What is of importance to this study is that in the church's understanding of itself and society, the papacy was by divine right the ruler of both the spiritual and temporal kingdoms. This self-understanding was codified in two documents that we will examine in some detail below. In both cases the claim of papal *principatus* is clear.

"The Donation of Constantine"

The story begins something like this: Four days after converting to Christianity, the Emperor Constantine gave Pope Sylvester and all popes to follow great lands and temporal power to rule even over the kings of nations and the emperor himself. Additionally, the pope was given the right to "make priest whomever he wishes, according to his own pleasure and counsel, and enroll him in the number of religious clergy ..., let no one whomsoever presume to act in a domineering way in this."[23] As a visible sign of this transfer of power, the emperor held the bridle of Sylvester's horse signifying the dominion of the sacred over the temporal.

The story ends this way: A humanist named Lorenzo Valla, in the mid-fifteenth century, unmasked the document known as *Constitum Constantini*, or the "Donation of Constantine," as a fake. According to Valla, the document which supposedly handed over temporal authority to the papacy and gave to the pope the exclusive right to ordain priests, had in fact been written sometime in the eighth century, some four hundred years after the death of Emperor Constantine.

For centuries, this document had been used as proof that all temporal authorities were subject to the authority of the pope, causing conflict and divisions in western Christendom. One example is the twelfth-century conflict between Emperor Frederick I and Pope Alexander III. In an attempt to install three anti-popes who would sanction his rule, Frederick had tried to make an end run around the authority of the pope to legitimize his reign. In the end, Alexander was triumphant and Frederick, following the supposed example of Constantine, showed

---

22. Ullmann, *Growth of Papal Government*, 451–52.
23. Valla, *Treatise of Lorenzo Valla*, 15.

his subservience to Alexander by helping the supreme pontiff onto his horse. Thus history showed that papal claims to temporal authority, following the dictates of the "Donation," were not to be challenged with impunity.

The Document

The document was included in Part 1, Division 96, Chapters 13 and 14 of Gratian's Decretum, or Harmony of the Canons, as well as in most medieval collections of canon law. It came to prominence in the ninth century after it was included in the Pseudo-Isodorian Decretals (c. 847–853).[24] In chapter 13 of Gratian's account of the Donation, the reader is informed that in the chapter to follow one will encounter how and why Constantine transferred spiritual and temporal power to Pope Sylvester by yielding "his crown, and all his royal prerogatives in the city of Rome, and in Italy, and in western parts to the Apostolic [See]."[25]

In chapter 14 the document reveals that the power of the pope was to be rooted in the reality that all Christian priests should regard Pope Sylvester and his successors as the head of the Church. The throne of the pontiff was to represent God's throne on earth and consequently "more than our empire and earthly throne the most sacred seat of the Blessed Peter shall be gloriously exalted, we giving to it power, and dignity of glory, and vigor, and honor imperial."[26]

In addition to an exalted throne, Constantine gives to Sylvester the signs and symbols of his imperial authority by declaring:

> we by this present do give our imperial Lateran palace, then the diadem, that is, the crown of our head, and at the same time the tiara and also the shoulder-band,—that is, the strap that usually surrounds our imperial neck; and also the purple mantle and scarlet tunic, and all the imperial raiment; and also the same rank as those presiding over the imperial cavalry, conferring also even the imperial scepters, and at the same time all the standards, and banners, and the different ornaments, and all the pomp of our imperial eminence, and the glory of our power.[27]

24. Ibid., 1.
25. Donation of Constantine, *Medieval Sourcebook*.
26. Ibid.
27. Ibid.

In order to make manifest the new privileges of the pontiff and his clerics, Constantine made provisions for a new style of dress that would signify the new-found authority of the clergy in Roman lands. In dress they are now to be adorned as one would expect a member of the Roman senate to be dressed. Yet it is not only the clergy who are to be singled out for special new garments, but their horses as well.

> And in order that the pontifical glory may shine forth most fully, we decree this also; that the horses of the clergy of this same holy Roman church be decorated with saddle-cloths and linens, that is, of the whitest color, and that they are to so ride. And even as our senate uses shoes with felt socks, that is, distinguished by white linen, so the clergy also should use them, so that, even as the celestial orders, so also the terrestrial may be adorned to the glory of God.

Most relevant to our study is the decree that follows the Emperor's insistence that clerics wear socks. The document reports that by imperial decree, the Roman pontiff alone has the authority to ordain priests.

> Above all things, moreover, we give permission to that same most holy one our Father Sylvester and to his successors, from our edict, that he may make priest whomever he wishes, according to his own pleasure and counsel, and enroll him in the number of the religious clergy [i.e., regular, or monastic, clergy; or, perhaps, the cardinals], let no one whomsoever presume to act in a domineering way in this.

Finally, Constantine is reported to have made this decree binding on all who follow him as emperor of Roman lands, and all those who occupy offices of temporal authority.

> Wherefore, before the living God who commanded us to reign, and in the face of his terrible judgment, we entreat, through this our imperial sanction, all the emperors our successors, and all the nobles, the satraps also, the most glorious senate, and all the people in the whole world, now and in all times still to come subject to our rule, that no one of them in any way be allowed either to break these [decrees], or in any way overthrow them.

It is argued that the "Donation" was produced sometime between the mid-eighth century and the mid-ninth century. Walter Ullmann makes a convincing argument that the document had to have existed before the blessing and anointing of Pippin (or Pepin), the father of

Charlemagne, as king in place of the Merovingians, in return for protection of the Holy See against the Lombards. Ullmann suspects that due to the language of the agreements between Pippin and the papacy there must have been a presupposition that the lands of Italy and the property that had been seized by the Lombards rightfully belonged to the papacy.

For example, in the agreements between Pippin and Pope Stephen II the words *reddere* and *restituere* are continually utilized when speaking of the return of the "whole exarchate and the people of Italy" to the pope. This language would have made absolutely no sense had there not been the assumption that these things did by right belong to the pope by a prior agreement, in this case, the "Donation." The fact that Pippin took upon himself the role of servant to the pope also seems to hearken to the language in the "Donation of Constantine."[28]

This period does indeed mark the beginning of movements by the Roman Curia to break away from subordination to imperial authority—particularly that of the Byzantine Empire—and negotiate with other secular authorities in order to secure their safety from those who would claim her wealth. Christopher Coleman makes similar claims in his introduction to *The Treatise of Lorenzo Valla on the Donation of Constantine*. Coleman correctly observes:

> The Papacy was then cutting loose from the Emperor at Constantinople and ignoring his representatives in Italy, as well as developing its own independent policy towards Italian territory, towards the Lombards, and towards the Franks. The aim of the forger seems to have been the characteristically medieval one of supplying documentary warrant for the existence of the situation which had developed through a long-drawn-out revolution, namely, the passage of imperial prerogatives and political control in Italy from the Emperor to the Papacy.[29]

The move by Pope Leo III to make Charlemagne emperor on Christmas Day 800 was certainly intended to assert that secular authority was given only with papal blessing. Though Charlemagne tried to assert his own authority when naming his son emperor, it was only when the pope officially crowned him as emperor that his rule was legitimated.

28. Ullmann, *Growth of Papal Government*, 58ff.
29. Valla, *Treatise of Lorenzo Valla*, 6.

Through these examples it is clear that the "Donation of Constantine" played a significant role in providing the papacy with the authority it needed to overcome the domination of secular rulers over the interests of the church. From the eighth century on, the pope was a temporal as well as a spiritual ruler in Europe, and the "Donation," forgery or not, played a role in establishing his power.

The "Donation" in Late Medieval Church Life: An Excursus

Though we will be concentrating on how the "Donation" was used to justify the subordination of temporal rulers to ecclesiastical officials, the "Donation" was also at the root of another controversy in the late Middle Ages. This controversy would impact how Luther was to regard the document in his writings and his reform program in "To the Christian Nobility of the German Nation."

In the late thirteenth and early fourteenth centuries many believed that the church must give up its wealth and follow the example of Christ and the first apostles, the example of voluntary poverty. As members of the church began to declare that the primary test of holiness was the commitment to a life of poverty, a doctrinal crisis ensued. If true Christian perfection was to be found only in imitation of the life of Christ and his apostles, what was to be said about the vast wealth of the Church?[30] Eventually, Pope John XXII declared that any teachings of Christ which called for a life of poverty were not binding on the Church.[31]

As the debate raged, some of the greatest thinkers of the day made their opinions known on the matter. William of Ockham declared that Pope John XXII's position on the poverty of Christ was heretical. For Ockham the possession of worldly goods did not immediately condemn a person as imperfect. Yet Christ's teaching to sell all possessions and follow him "laid down the definition of 'perfection' for all who would strive after it in the church."[32] Pelikan notes that all this attention towards poverty in the church could very well have been an attempt by

---

30. Pelikan, *Reformation of the Church*, 87.
31. Ibid., 88.
32. Ibid., 89.

many, with the support of temporal rulers, to redistribute the wealth accumulated by the church.[33]

The "Donation of Constantine" stood at the center of this debate as it was with the conversion of Constantine, and his support of the church, that the inheritors of the apostolic tradition came to prominence, power and great wealth. It was the "Donation," or more specifically the tradition behind the "Donation," which gave as legal right great wealth to the pope and his church. The Hussite Jacoubek ze Stříbra claimed that the "Donation" was the work of the devil, though he was willing to concede that Constantine had the best of intentions when he decided to grant such power to the pope. Dante contended that the pope had no right to accept such a gift from the emperor, nor did the emperor have the right to grant such a gift. Ockham cited the Donation as proof that the church received its authority from the state, not the other way around.[34]

On the other hand, the "Donation" was used by those who supported the positions of the pope as confirmation that the church had the right and obligation to maintain its wealth and power. Conrad of Megenberg went so far as to claim that until Constantine made his Donation and was baptized, he could not be considered an emperor because his reign applied only to that which was outside the church. The "Donation" was understood by moderates in the debate as a gift from God. "The Donation did not prove that what the emperor had was originally the property of the pope; it did prove that temporal possessions did not eo ipso corrupt the holiness of the church, and that the pope should share his wealth with the church."[35]

Some of these arguments find expression in Luther's own writings. In his commentary on Isaiah 61:8 Luther stated:

> Almost all have twisted this text so as to apply to the peace of the church granted in the time of Constantine who adorned the church. This adornment is not to honor the church but to be onerous to it, as it is written in that time that a voice was heard to say in the Lateran Church: "Now poison has been injected into the church." It is not proper for it to rule, and to govern in an external way hinders the office of the Word, as we have experienced.[36]

---

33. Ibid., 89.
34. Pelikan, *Reformation of the Church*, 90.
35. Ibid., 91.
36. LW 17:338.

And again, "But today the word "treasure" has a different meaning so that men no longer speak of the poor as the treasures of the church. With this word we refer to the patrimony of Christ and St. Peter, chaff without grain, as it were, which Constantine has given to the church."[37]

In "To the Christian Nobility of the German Nation," Luther attacks the legitimacy of papal claims by attacking the legitimacy of the Donation itself. In so doing he pushes the debate over church—more specifically, papal—privilege by challenging not only the right of the church to possess wealth, but temporal power as well.

The Papal Bull *Unam Sanctam*

Even if the "Donation of Constantine" had been proven a forgery, Pope Leo X had reason to feel confident in his claim that he wielded power as both spiritual and temporal sovereign in the West. At the Council of Rome, 1517, Leo re-issued the papal bull *Unam Sanctam* in a new bull *Pastor Aeternus*.[38] *Unam Sanctam* was a continuation of the development of papal claims of *plenitudo potestatis* which would find its completion in late medieval papal hierocratic theory.[39] Thus it is an important document in the understanding of the development of the medieval cosmology that was eventually attacked by Luther's universal priesthood.

In the penultimate month of the year 1302, the papal bull, *Unam Sanctam*, or One Holy—in reference to the church—was made public. In it, Pope Boniface VIII attempted to put to rest any speculation concerning the nature of papal authority. The bull was promulgated in response to an ongoing conflict between the Pope and King Philip IV of France, also called the Fair.

The conflict between the King and Pontiff began when the King attempted to levy taxes against the clergy in his domain. In reaction against this new tax, the Pope issued the bull *Clericis Laicos* (1296), forbidding any of his priests to submit to the taxation. In response, the King forbade the exporting of coins from his land, taking away a valu-

---

37. LW 31:228.

38. Ullmann, *Growth of Papal Government*, 456 n. 2. Harold Grimm, in his notes to Luther's "Proceedings at Augsburg" contends that the bull was actually issued at the Fifth Lateran Council on January 14, 1516. LW 31:262 n. 7.

39. McCready, "Papal Plenitudo Potestatis," 659.

able source of revenue for the papal curia. Following the imprisonment of a papal legate by King Philip, Boniface issued his now famous bull which subordinated the temporal powers to the spiritual estate.

The bull itself drew upon a variety of sources. Its teachings reflected an ecclesiology already expressed by Bernard, Hugh of St. Victor, Cyprian and Thomas Aquinas. It has also been suggested that the document reflected pseudo-Denis the Aeropagite in its references to questions related to the location of the state of perfection within the hierarchy of the church.[40]

> We are informed by the texts of the gospels that in this Church and in its power are two swords; namely, the spiritual and the temporal. For when the Apostles say: 'Behold, here are two swords' [Lk 22:38] that is to say, in the Church, since the Apostles were speaking, the Lord did not reply that there were too many, but sufficient. Certainly the one who denies that the temporal sword is in the power of Peter has not listened well to the word of the Lord commanding: 'Put up thy sword into thy scabbard' [Mt 26:52]. Both, therefore, are in the power of the Church, that is to say, the spiritual and the material sword, but the former is to be administered for [sic] the Church but the latter by [sic] the Church; the former in the hands of the priest; the latter by the hands of kings and soldiers, but at the will and sufferance of the priest.
>
> However, one sword ought to be subordinated to the other and temporal authority, subjected to spiritual power. For since the Apostle said: 'There is no power except from God and the things that are, are ordained of God' [Rom 13:1–2], but they would not be ordained if one sword were not subordinated to the other and if the inferior one, as it were, were not led upwards by the other.[41]

The need for a new bull articulating papal authority was not simply a reaction to a single incident, or set of incidents. There was increased interest on the part of scholars in the role of the national ruler's function and position in relation to the papacy based on ideas of secularization which had begun to be expressed in the twelfth century. Movements which resurrected the ancient Roman understanding of government recognized the role emperors once played in ruling and in determining

---

40. Luscombe, "'Lex Divinitatis,'" 205.
41. Pope Boniface VIII, "Unam Sanctam," Medieval Sourcebook.

church doctrine. The argument that the kings once had full and unobstructed power to rule over their lands and the church constituted a real threat to a cosmology which relied on the universality of the Christian body under the authority of the pope and the papal government. As a result, "scholarship and governmental practice combined promoted a national governmental outlook, that is, territorial sovereignty, with a consequential diminution of the universal papal jurisdiction."[42]

Such brilliant minds as William of Ockham and Marsilius of Padua spoke out against the claim that the pope had any authority outside the confines of the spiritual lives of the church. Ockham stressed the freedom of all Christian believers and revived the distinction between the temporal and spiritual powers. In his mind, the pope had no jurisdiction over the emperor.

Marsilius of Padua argued that the state was the sole supporter of peace. The church operates as only one part of the whole of society and is part of the state in secular matters. Because secular law is distinct from divine law, the church is to leave governing the people to those who are better equipped to defend the law and the state. The pope derives his authority from the whole body of Christians and to some extent is subject by his office to that community. He also went on to question whether the pope could claim superiority over the other members of the Christian clergy.[43]

The bull *Unam Sanctam* is Boniface's attempt to bring the debate over these issues back to the arena of cosmology. Based on the great minds of the past, Boniface intended to remind his contemporaries that much more was at stake than the simple matter of papal authority. For the pope, the structures of the church and the world are a reflection of God's will and God's very nature. One of the great minds that Boniface apparently relied on heavily was pseudo-Denis. Denis was cited regularly in thirteenth-century polemics which attempted a description of the nature of the church and the location of the state of perfection within ecclesiastical hierarchy.[44] One finds certain reference to Denis in *Unam Sanctam*

---

42. Ullmann, "Boniface VIII," 71.
43. Grimm, *Reformation Era*, 30–31.
44. Luscombe, "'Lex Divinitatis,'" 205.

> For, according to the Blessed Dionysius, it is a law of the divinity that the lowest things reach the highest place by intermediaries. Then, according to the order of the universe, all things are not led back to order equally and immediately, but the lowest by the intermediary, and the inferior by the superior. Hence we must recognize the more clearly that spiritual power surpasses in dignity and in nobility any temporal power whatever, as spiritual things surpass the temporal.[45]

Denis had suggested that the celestial hierarchy was to be a model for the church as it was ordered on earth. This was the *lex divinitatis*, or the law of divinity, which compelled society to reflect the divine ordering of the body of Christ. The hierarchic ordering of creation, which can be found in the Trinity itself, constitutes a law of order which provides the resemblance between God and the created order.[46]

Contemporaries of Boniface, such as James of Viterbo, professor of theology at the University of Paris and then Archbishop of Benevento and Archbishop of Naples, argued that the church was the fulfillment of the kingdom of God on earth and as such should be understood as the primary kingdom of the world. And if the church is the kingdom of God, then the pope is also the kingdom of God's vicar on earth. If Christ is king and priest, his vicar is both king and priest as well. It is through Christ and his vicar that royal power is instituted and ordered.[47]

The concept of medieval hierocratic theory, as articulated by thinkers like James of Viterbo, interpreted the doctrines related to papal power and papal authority as a culmination of three basic assumptions. First, Christ, even as a human, possessed both priestly and royal power. Second, the sole Vicar of Christ on earth is the Roman pope. Finally, the pope, as a consequence of the first two suppositions, possesses Christ's kingly and priestly authority. Because Christ was understood as lord of all creation, he would be denying himself if he were to admit that anyone is exempt from his spiritual or temporal authority. In the same way, if the pope would claim that anyone is exempt from his spiritual or temporal authority, he would be denying that he is the true Vicar of Christ.[48]

---

45. Pope Boniface VIII, "*Unam Sanctam*," *Medieval Sourcebook*.
46. Luscombe, "'*Lex Divinitatis*,'" 207.
47. Pelikan, *Reformation of the Church*, 82.
48. McCready, "Papal Plenitudo Potestatis," 660.

Thus, *Unam Sanctam*, far from being a radical step towards papal domination of secular powers, was a document that based its arguments on a view of hierarchy which had been present throughout the Middle Ages and in particular reflected the work done by many in the thirteenth century to reassert the rationale behind papal government in the face of a new form of nationalism. This all comes to a head in the distinction between clerical and lay power.[49]

As Luther articulated his universal priesthood, he attacked the heart of papal authority on temporal matters—an attack with well-known consequences. The papal bull made clear the teachings of the church on these matters:

> Therefore whoever resists this power thus ordained by God, resists the ordinance of God [Rom 13:2], unless he invent like Manicheus two beginnings, which is false and judged by us heretical, since according to the testimony of Moses, it is not in the beginnings but in the beginning that God created heaven and earth [Gen 1:1]. Furthermore, we declare, we proclaim, we define that it is absolutely necessary for salvation that every human creature be subject to the Roman Pontiff.[50]

Luther's reactions to the provisions of *Unam Sanctam* were predictable. In his 1519 commentary on Galatians, Luther had challenged the notion in *Unam Sanctam* that the pope has no judge on earth as all others do, saying, "certain heralds of Antichrist have reached the point that they prate in the foulest manner that no one is allowed to say—especially not to the Roman pontiff—"Why are you doing this?" Furthermore, they prate that the pope has no judge on earth, and that Christ would not have provided adequately for His church if He had not assigned to a human being such great power as this man has."[51] In his sermon on 2 Peter (1523), in particular 2:11, Luther spoke with perfect candor concerning the supposed doctrine of two swords.

> [Peter] calls kings, princes, lords, and all worldly government, not the popes and the bishops, "authority," for the latter were not to be lords, since Christ appointed only servants in the New Testament. One Christian was to serve and honor the other Christian. Therefore Peter means that they should be subject

---

49. Luscombe, "The '*Lex Divinitatis*,'" 208.
50. Pope Boniface VIII, "*Unam Sanctam,*" *Medieval Sourcebook*.
51. LW 27:342.

and obedient to the secular overlords, in order that the sword, which is instituted by God's arrangement, might be feared. But they do the very opposite; they have excluded themselves and say that they are not subject to the secular government. Yes, they have not only excluded themselves; but they have also subjected the secular government to themselves and have trodden it underfoot. Brazenly they let themselves be called lords even by kings and princes, just as the pope writes about himself that he is lord of heaven and earth, that he has both the spiritual and the secular sword in his hand, and that everyone is obliged to fall down before him.[52]

Again, much later in his life, in his commentary on Genesis 49:11–12 (1545) he declared "the pope makes the impudent and proud boast: 'The emperor's sword is in my hand; and although it is in the emperor's sheath, yet he does not dare draw it except with my permission.'"[53]

Luther's attacks on the authority of the pope were by their very nature radical *and* political. They were radical because they went to the root of papal authority and supremacy which, though often lamented, were firmly established and maintained through force of arms, if necessary. They were political because they sought a re-ordering of political power, shifting temporal authority away from Rome and placing it firmly in the hands of those who held rank only in the temporal estate.

These attacks were welcomed by many who had similar convictions. In time Luther's voice was joined to others who had for many years made the same claims, though not quite so radically as Luther.

Challenges to Papal Authority

Investituture Controversy

Perhaps the most well-documented conflict over the concept of priestly *auctoritas* to precede the early modern German Reformation is the Investiture Controversy of the eleventh and early twelfth centuries in Germany. As evidenced by the Investiture Controversy, the lay opposition to the hierocratic scheme was above all governmentally concentrated in the emperors. The imperial thesis, as far as it was capable of formulating an independent theory of its own, naturally became the fo-

52. LW 30:180.
53. LW 8:264.

cal point of anti-hierocratic opposition.[54] It is not surprising that Luther calls upon the emperor as the last hope for reformation of the church. As is the case throughout Luther's career, he put his own particular stamp on ideas that had been developed by others before him.

The term investiture was used to designate the act and the ceremonies by which princes granted to church prelates the possessions which constituted their benefices[55] and the political rights which they were to exercise. Under Pope Gregory VII, the practice of lay people investing church leaders with titles and authority was challenged. The issue of investitures was important for civil authorities because the church and her servants had become so powerful that they were potentially political threats. The issue was equally important for the pope and church leaders because the possessions of the church—along with the claims of spiritual authority which exceeded the claims of the temporal authorities—could not be relinquished to temporal powers.[56]

Emperor Henry IV believed that he must be able to control the appointments of bishops and church prelates because their power had become so significant. For the Emperor the matter would determine the political survival of the empire itself.[57] Yet the Pope's authority was also challenged on theological grounds by such thinkers as the so-called Anonymous of York.[58]

His argument was rooted in his understanding of the historical development of papal authority and Christology. According to the

---

54. Ullmann, *Growth of Papal Government*, 453.

55. A benefice is a spiritual office to which the church has attached the perpetual right to gather revenues (or annates). The assessment of the income for each benefice was referred to as its *taxatio*. The taxes for each benefice were determined by papal assessors on the basis of local inquests. See Phillip H. Stump, "The Reform of Papal Taxation at the Council of Constance (1414–1418)." *Speculum* 64.1 (1989) 73. These benefices are dealt with specifically by Luther in *To the Christian Nobility of the German Nation* and will be explored in more detail below.

56. Gonzalez, *Story of Christianity*, 291.

57. Ibid., 286.

58. The term Anonymous of York, in actuality, refers to a group of tractates published in the early twelfth century. These tractates dealt with church-state relations. They were compiled and published together in 1899 by Heinrich Böhmer, who ascribed sole authorship of the documents to the figure called the Anonymous of York, a figure he assumed was Gerard, the Archbishop of York. The authorship of the document has been questioned by George Williams in his work *The Norman Anonymous of 1100 A.D.* George Williams, *The Norman Anonymous of 1100 A.D.*, Harvard Theological Studies, XVII (Cambridge, MA, 1951).

Anonymous of York, the pope had received his position of authority from the church Fathers, not from God, and thus the papacy was not a reflection of the divine ordering of creation. Instead, the papacy was an institution with its origins in history. Additionally, he posited, the city of Rome itself was chosen as the center of the church world because of its position as the capital of the world, not because of its links to the apostle Peter. There was no such thing as papal *plenitudo potestatis* because there was no such thing as primacy in the early church, and Christ said nothing concerning this kind of authority. Christ had given all the apostles equal power and each bishop is the successor of Peter. If one church or church authority is by nature superior to others, then two churches are made from one and the one indivisible church is divided.[59]

Imperialist thinkers also denied the pope's authority over the emperors by citing Romans 13. The emperor was a representative of God. Even if the king is a lay person, by his consecration he is elevated to the priestly role. Gregory of Catino claimed that because the emperor is anointed with holy oil he should be given the status as the Lord's anointed.[60]

Hugh of Fleury theorized that within the boundaries of his kingdom, the king takes upon himself the role of God the Father, and the bishops assume the role of Christ, the Son. For this reason, all bishops should be subordinate to the king as Christ is subordinate to the Father. The so-called Anonymous of York continued this line of reasoning by asserting that the king embodies the divine nature of Christ, while the priests embody the human nature of Christ. Christ was both king and priest, but the royal nature in Christ was higher than the priestly.[61]

The issue of lay investiture came to a head when the emperor deposed the Bishop of Milan. Pope Gregory ordered Henry to appear before him to answer for his intrusion into church matters and added that if the Emperor refused to comply with his summons the Emperor would be excommunicated. In January 1076, Henry IV responded in kind by "deposing" Gregory VII as Pope. In his letter to Gregory, he referred to him by his birth name writing, "Henry, king not through usurpation but through the holy ordination of God, to Hildebrand, at present not pope but false monk." He continues with his complaint:

59. Tellenbach, *Church, State*, 146.
60. Ibid., 149.
61. Ibid., 149.

"... thou, however, hast understood our humility to be fear, and hast not, accordingly, shunned to rise up against the royal power conferred upon us by God, daring to threaten to divest us of it. As if we had received our kingdom from thee! As if the kingdom and the empire were in thine and not in God's hand!"[62]

The papal response was predictable. In February 1076, drawing upon the notion of papal *principitus*, Gregory declared,

> ... especially to me, as [God's] representative and by [God's] favour, has the power been granted by God of binding and loosing in Heaven and on earth. On the strength of this belief therefore, for the honour and security of thy church, in the name of Almighty God, Father, Son and Holy Ghost, I withdraw, through thy power and authority, from Henry the king, son of Henry the emperor, who has risen against thy church with unheard of insolence, the rule over the whole kingdom of the Germans and over Italy.[63]

Eventually a formal agreement was reached at the Concordat of Worms in 1122 and the path towards reconciliation was chosen. According to the Concordat, the church alone would have the right to invest prelates with their authority. Emperor Henry V promised

> In the name of the holy and indivisible Trinity, I, Henry, by the grace of God august emperor of the Romans, for the love of God and of the holy Roman church and of our master pope Calixtus, and for the healing of my soul, do remit to God, and to the holy apostles of God, Peter and Paul, and to the holy catholic church, all investiture through ring and staff; and do grant that in all the churches that are in my kingdom or empire there may be canonical election and free consecration.[64]

However, the right of the church officials to serve as feudal lords was to be granted by civil authorities. Yet, in the final analysis, the source of authority was to be found in the papacy.

---

62. Henderson, *Select Historical Documents*, 372.
63. Ibid., 376–77.
64. Ibid., 408–9.

The Conciliar Movement

During the fourteenth and fifteenth centuries the authority of the papacy was again called into question in what is now called the conciliar movement. Though the issues that gave rise to the movement were not specifically about the relationship between secular and spiritual authority the controversy did occasion another opportunity to consider the claims of papal power. Luther drew on the conclusions of many in the conciliar movement when he penned "To the Christian Nobility of the German Nation" and adopted the viewpoints of those who advocated council authority over popes.

Conciliarism was not one unified movement. It had many expressions. However, most conciliarists held to some form of the idea that the church was a corporate body. Although the church has an earthly head, the pope, the power of the church was rooted in the head of the mystical body, Christ. The universal church, which constituted the body of Christ, was the source of power which was granted to the pope with limits. In the final analysis, all those impacted by a law had the right to give input about how the law is formulated.[65]

The most radical of the conciliarists held that the highest authority in the church was the general council. Yet others believed that the councils and the pope should be considered partners. However, even those who advocated shared authority only allowed the pope to claim a delegated authority over administrative matters. As for the College of Cardinals, they held the opinion that because the Cardinals choose the pope they were *de facto* part of the body of the papacy and shared papal authority.[66]

Christopher Bellitto suggests that the roots of the conciliar movement can be found in the monastic orders. The structure of the monasteries, with the abbot serving as head of the body, was rooted in a decision made by the monks themselves as to who would rule over them. Thus, it was the body that gave authority to the head. From this line of reasoning, the body has the right to demand an accounting of the head. However, he also points back to the apostolic tradition found in the book of Acts. The Council of Jerusalem was not called by a pope, and it was not led by a pope. Additionally, the Councils of Nicaea,

---

65. Bellitto, *General Councils*, 82.
66. Ibid., 83.

Constantinople, and Ephesus were called when papal authority was almost nonexistent.[67]

Though Bellitto's comments are accurate, perhaps a more precise location of the roots of conciliarism is identified by Matthew Spinka in his introduction found in *John Hus at the Council of Constance*.[68] His work is of particular importance to this study because it attempts to link the conciliar movement to the reformation movements which directly impacted Luther. Furthermore, the condemnation of Hus by the Council of Constance was addressed by Luther specifically in "To the Christian Nobility of the German Nation."

Spinka suggests that the principle source for conciliar theory was Gratian's *Decretum*. The *Decretum* was a compilation of close to 4,000 texts compiled by the Benedictine monk Gratian in the middle of the twelfth century. The text became a foundational document used by canonists for teaching and expounding upon canon law. The early canonists developed the theories which informed the conciliarists. "The chief concern of the canonists was to make the *congregatio fidelium* superior to the rapidly growing pretensions of the papacy to the absolute authority within the Church."[69] This is most evidenced by the work of Huguccio (d. 1210), the great decretist and teacher of Pope Innocent III, who distinguished between the power inherent in the universal church and the authority that could be exercised by the pope.

The conciliarists developed the ideas of the decretists, beginning with the work of John of Paris. John of Paris, a Dominican (d. 1302) defines the church as one Christian people, one mystical body which is not Peter but Christ. The head of the Church militant is the pope; yet the office is administrative and limited to the spiritual realm. In an argument that foreshadows Luther's own claims in "To the Christian Nobility of the German Nation," John makes the claim that the temporal government also derives its power from God. John argued that because the church is a corporation the power is diffused amongst its members.[70]

Marsilius of Padua (1275–1347?), in his *Defensor pacis*, made the claim that the church is defined by the whole body, not the pope. Christ

67. Ibid.
68. Spinka, trans., *John Hus*.
69. Ibid., 4.
70. Ibid.

is the head. The highest tribunal is the council. It is the council, not the pope, that controls excommunications, elects priests, defines articles of faith, and finally elects the pope. Marsilius went on to make the claim that the council is infallible because it is led by the Spirit. Prior to Marsilius, only John of Paris had made this claim.[71]

Marsilius, using Aristotle as his guide, commented next on the organization of the church. He claimed that the body possessed essential and accidental aspects. The essential aspects of the church were derived from God; the accidental aspects were derived from human appointment. The essential aspects were shared by the entire priesthood. Of importance to this study is what Marsilius considered to be accidental aspects of the church. Among them was the distinction of office, which he held to be of human origin. Finally, he limited the use of coercive authority to the political powers.[72]

William of Ockham (d. 1349) distinguished between the universal church and the Roman church as a species. Christ is head of the universal church.[73] This church cannot err. Yet the head of the Roman church can err. Additionally, the universal church alone has the power to appoint a vice-regent. Surprisingly, this vice-regent is not the pope, but the general council! However, contrary to Marsilius, Ockham believed councils can err.[74] The authority given to the pope by the council can only be expressed in the spiritual realm. The temporal powers possess rule over temporalities by divine authority.[75]

The next stage of conciliarist thought was occasioned by the great schism. During much of the fourteenth century many of the popes resided in Avignon, France. Shortly after moving the Holy See back to Rome in 1378, Pope Gregory XI died and there was a dispute over who would replace him as pope. Because of this dispute a group of church leaders set up an anti-pope back in Avignon and the period from 1378–1417 became known as the great Western schism. Those in the conciliar movement hoped to heal this division in the church and the

71. Ibid., 6.
72. Ibid.
73. Ibid., 9.
74. Ibid., 10.
75. Ibid., 11.

abuses which provided the sub-text for the division without making any significant change in Roman dogma.[76]

Proponents of the conciliar movement believed that a universal council which represented the entire church had more authority than a pope. Thus the question of the legitimacy of any pope could be settled by the council, and there was no need to rely on individual popes to legitimize their authority through political means.[77]

After the great schism, the most eloquent proponents of conciliarism were found in the faculty of the University of Paris. The foundations of their arguments can be located in the ideas of Conrad of Gelnhausen (1320–1390) who introduced the concept of *epikeia* into the debate over the authority of the councils over the pope. *Epikeia* was a concept by which ordinary canonical provisions might be superseded if necessary. The concept of *epikeia* is simple enough on the surface. The idea is that when extraordinary events force the church to reconsider the application of a law the church can, for a time, suspend the law because the circumstance could not have been foreseen by the originator of the law or rule. Thus, any law which held that the pope alone had authority to call a council could be set aside during times of conflict, especially when the conflict is caused by the pope himself.[78] This idea becomes a thread that runs through the arguments of many of the most prominent conciliarists of the fifteenth century.

Pierre d'Ailly (1350–1420) was a disciple of William of Ockham and served as chancellor of the University of Paris. He wrote the satirical *Epistola diaboli Leviathan* which was a letter from the Devil calling on the church to fight the general council. The Devil, according to the work, loves the disunity. Eventually d'Ailly became a bishop and supported the calling of the councils.[79] He argued that the church, as the mystical body of Christ, had—according to the *Decretum*—the authority to call a council. He further argued that in matters of necessity the positive laws must give place to the principle of *epikeia*.

In 1411 he was made a cardinal but still maintained conciliarist principles at the Council of Constance. He held that the concept of inerrancy was to be found only in the body of Christ; popes and councils

---

76. Gonzalez, *Story of Christianity*, 342.
77. Ibid., 343.
78. Spinka, *John Hus*, 12.
79. Ibid., 13.

can, and have erred. In the final analysis, the pope could only hold supremacy within a council, but never over the council.[80]

Jean Charlier de Gerson (1363–1429) succeeded d'Ailly as chancellor of the University of Paris. He too held to the notion that the mystical body of Christ has the power to secure its own unity by exercising authority over the leadership of the church, especially the pope.[81]

Prior to the Council of Pisa he argued that the Council had sufficient authority to invoke the *epikeia*. In his 1409 *Tractatus de unitate ecclesiastica* he wrote: "the unity of the Church in one vicar of Christ does not require for its attainment at the present time a literal observance of the outward terms of positive law . . . This general Council may proceed summarily, and with the good and important [principle] of equity. It shall have sufficient judicial authority to use the *epikeia*."[82]

Francesco Zabarella (1360–1417) was the cardinal-deacon of Florence and considered one of the most distinguished canonists of his time. His ideas concerning the authority of the universal church to call a council directly impact our examination of Luther's "To the Christian Nobility of the German Nation."

In his *Tractatus de schismate*, Zabarella borrowed heavily from the decretists, including John of Paris. In it he described the church as a corporation presided over by the pope. Yet the concept of the universal church served as the source of authority. In the context of the schism, the General Council was the best vehicle for dealing with schism and was best suited to determine how the authority of the church should be made manifest in the office of the pope. He declared that canon law gives the pope the right to call a council, but that right devolves to cardinals if the pope fails to call a council when necessary.[83]

However, if the College of Cardinals fails to exercise its authority in a time of crisis the authority to call a council falls to the emperor as the representative of the people, an idea that will be expanded upon by Luther in "To the Christian Nobility of the German Nation." Thus, papal power was founded on power conferred by the body.[84]

---

80. Ibid., 14.
81. Ibid., 17.
82. Quoted in ibid., 18.
83. Ibid., 20.
84. Ibid.

Despite the apparent end of the Great Schism, Martin V called yet another council in 1423. Though it was originally scheduled to meet in Pavia, the council was moved to Sienna in order to escape the impact of the plague. This particular council failed to accomplish much in the way of reform.

Through a series of councils beginning in Pisa in 1409, conciliarists and their supporters sought to bring an end to the divisions of the church. The council that met in Pisa enjoyed the support of the College of Cardinals and a great deal of the courts in Europe. The council decided not to try and solve the question of which pope was legitimate and declared that both popes were unworthy of the office. The council deposed both and elected Alexander V to the office of pontiff.

However, as could be expected, the other claimants to the pontificate were not willing to recognize the authority of the council. Thus the church now had three popes. After the death of Alexander V the cardinals elected a new pope, John XXIII. John was forced to flee Rome and sought the protection of Emperor Sigismund of Germany. Sigismund decided that another council was needed to put an end to the divisions in the church and persuaded John to make such a council a reality.

The new council gathered in Constance in 1414 and John expected to be backed by those in attendance. However, many cardinals did not appreciate John's opulent lifestyle and to his surprise the council demanded his resignation. Eventually John abdicated and Martin V was elected pope. The Avignon pope, Benedict XIII died in 1423 and was not replaced, and the third pope, Gregory XII, resigned.

The Council at Constance is best known for condemning the teachings of John Hus, but the council was largely unable to reform the church in other ways. Simony and other similar practices would need to be dealt with at another time. The final decision of the council was to order the convening of similar councils on a regular basis to make certain that the reform of the church would continue. The stipulation published under the title *Frequens* dictated that,

> Therefore, by a perpetual edict, we sanction, decree, establish and ordain that general councils shall be celebrated in the following manner, so that the next one shall follow the close of this present council at the end of five years. The second shall follow the close of that, at the end of seven years, and councils shall thereafter be celebrated every ten years in such places as the

Pope shall be required to designate and assign, with the consent and approbation of the council, one month before the close of the council in question, or which, in his absence, the council itself shall designate.[85]

Pope Martin V was weary of councils but understood that he could do little to avoid them, and eventually another council was scheduled for 1430. That council met in Basel. As for the pope, his wish to avoid yet another council was granted when death took him shortly after the council gathered. The gathering of leaders elected Eugene IV as pope. Eugene declared the council dissolved, but the council refused to disband and contemplated taking action against Eugene. Only after the intervention of Emperor Sigismund did Eugene withdraw his declaration of dissolution. It appeared that the council had finally won the battle in the war of supremacy over the church.

Events would come to favor the pope in a very short period of time. While the council was meeting, a request came from the Eastern Church. The Byzantine emperor and the patriarch of Constantinople called on the Western powers for help in their defense against the Turks. The Eastern Church declared that it was ready to rejoin the fold so long as the council was moved nearer to Constantinople. Eugene leapt at the chance to unify the church and at the same time regain his authority over her councils. He declared that the council would move to Ferrara. Most of the council agreed to the move but some remained in Basel. Thus, the council was now divided. The remaining delegates in Basel elected a new pope and in so doing created a new rupture in the church. This rebellious council and its pope finally gave into the reality that they were helpless; they disbanded and the antipope resigned. It now seemed that the pope and the papacy had won the day.

The apparent victory of pontiff over councils was codified in 1459 by Pope Pius II in his decree *Execrabilis*, in which he labeled the conciliarists and their movement erroneous and detestable.

> The execrable and hitherto unknown abuse has grown up in our day, that certain persons, imbued with the spirit of rebellion and not from a desire to secure a better judgment, but to escape the punishment of some offence which they have committed, presume to appeal from the pope to a future council, in spite of the fact that the pope is the vicar of Jesus Christ and to him, in

85. *Frequens, Medieval Sourcebook*.

the person Peter, the following was said: "Feed my sheep" [John 21:16] and "Whatsoever thou shalt bind on earth shall be bound in heaven" [Matt. 16:18]. Wishing therefore to expel this pestiferous poison from the church of Christ and to care for the salvation of the fold entrusted to us, and to remove every cause of offence from the fold of our Saviour, with the advice and consent of our brothers, the cardinals of the holy Roman church, and of all the prelates, and of those who have been trained in the canon and civil law, who are at our court, and with our own sure knowledge, we condemn all such appeals and prohibit them as erroneous and detestable.[86]

Gravamina of the German Nation

By the late Middle Ages, the chief form of protest used by Germans to present grievances to the Roman church was the *gravamina*.[87] In particular, the *gravamina* had become a tool in the fight against papal authority. During the Council of Constance (1414–1418), German representatives presented eighteen directives which they believed would free their people from what they considered to be abuses of papal power, including the selling of indulgences. Similar grievances regarding papal taxation were also presented at the Council of Basel (1431–1449).

In "To the Christian Nobility of the German Nation," Luther joined the principles of reform in both the spiritual and political realms.[88] The call for reform of the church, as it related to the political realities of the Holy Roman Empire and Germany in particular, had been made in the form of the *Gravamina nationis germanicae* many years before anyone heard the name Martin Luther. These *gravamina* consisted of German national complaints against certain practices of the church and those who represented the church in Germany. They were frequently referred and directed to Rome in hopes of alleviating some of the burdens carried by the German churches.[89] Yet it was Luther who added the authority of the evangelical faith and his own person to these grievances. In order to

---

86. Pope Pius II, "*Execrabilis*," *Medieval Sourcebook*.

87. *Gravamina* is the plural of *gravamen,* a late, and rather uncommon, Latin noun meaning trouble, annoyance, physical inconvenience, or burden.

88. Gebhardt, *Die gravamina*, 93.

89. Strauss, ed. and trans., *Manifestations of Discontent*, 35.

contextualize Luther's call for spiritual and temporal reforms, we must first examine the work upon which he built his political manifesto.

The *gravamina* are essentially inner-church proposals. Indeed, most of the *gravamina* were leveled at the pope by the higher clergy. For example, in or around 1447, the chancellor to the Archbishop of Mainz, Martin Mair, sent a letter to the newly appointed cardinal Enea Silvio Piccolomini (who would later become Pope Pius II), expressing concerns about abuses suffered by the German church. Though the original copy of Mair's letter has been lost, an overview of his arguments still survives as part of Piccolomini's reply to Mair. From this text, the nature of the German grievances is clear. Complaints against Pope Calixtus III claim that he was determined to bleed the German nation dry. Deserving to be quoted at length, Mair, through the cardinal's summary, described the problems facing the church:

> Elections of prelates are set aside. Benefices and incomes of all kinds are reserved to cardinals and protonotaries; you yourself [Piccolomini] are the holder of reservations of benefices in three German provinces. Expectancies[90] are granted in unlimited numbers. Annates or semi-annual revenues are collected without thought of respite, and everyone knows how much more is squeezed out than we owe. Clerical positions are given not to those best qualified to hold them but to the highest bidders. New indulgences are approved day after day for one purpose only: their profits to Rome. Turkish tithes are levied without so much as a by-your-leave to our own prelates. Law suites that should plainly be heard in our own courts are summarily transferred to Rome. A thousand subtle tricks are invented to cheat us "barbarians" out of our money.[91]

Wishing to make the consequences of such abuses clear, Mair warned the cardinal that the temporal authorities were beginning to "wake up" and could eventually take these matters into their own hands, perhaps leading them to "shake off their yoke, and regain the ancient freedom they have lost."[92] Cardinal Piccolomini's response was to be expected. He claimed, "The grievances and burdens catalogued by Mair either do not exist or are trivial . . . Papal fiscal practices, though uni-

---

90. An expectancy is the appointment to a church office before it has been vacated. See ibid., 38 n. 3.

91. Ibid., 38.

92. Ibid.

versally maligned, are in fact efficient and, by and large, honest. Abuses do exist, but pope and cardinals are men, after all, and will occasionally fall victim to human failings . . . You are jealous of the money going to Rome; there you have the root of your accusation."[93] Piccolomini's response made clear the inability of the Roman church to clean its own house, a factor that Lohse concludes led to the realization among many in the sixteenth century that true reform would not have been possible from within the church structure.[94] In his reply concerning the potential rebellion of the German princes against the pontiff, Piccolomini has no conception of the possibility that one day a wild boar will arise in Wittenberg. "Contemplating rebellion against Rome is folly. Who are these "leaders" you say are making preparations to "oppose" Rome? It is only the rabble, the mob, that craves "innovations" and talks revolution. What ingratitude! Where would you be without the Roman Church, the "Mother of the German people?" You would be heathens still."[95]

Around 1451, a German clergyperson, perhaps a member of the lower clergy, or a monk compiled a list of grievances to coincide with Nicholas of Cusa's (1400/01–1464) trip to Germany.[96] It is assumed that the text was forwarded to him at the Synod of Mainz in 1451.[97]

The first call was for a general council or a German national council to be convened in order to deal with the perceived abuses suffered by the German churches. Included among these abuses were the granting of ecclesiastical benefices through simony and inflated fees for awards of expectancies.

In addition, the author of these *gravamina* was offended at the practice of granting reservations to benefices that were not even vacant. The familiar refrain of the opulence of the curia was also voiced.[98]

The sale of Jubilee Indulgences provided the author with an occasion to articulate German nationalistic sentiments: "Why should

---

93. Ibid., 39.

94. Lohse, *Introduction*, 10.

95. Strauss, *Manifestations of Discontent*, 40.

96. Nicholas of Cusa was a German-born Cardinal and canon lawyer. He was made a Cardinal by Pope Nicholas V and was eventually appointed bishop of Brixten. He served the pope as an envoy to Germany.

97. Strauss, *Manifestations of Discontent*, 48.

98. Ibid., 50.

Germans be victimized when Italians make huge profits by pocketing the proceeds from the Jubilee Year ... ?"[99]

Church leaders continued their protest of extreme fiscal pressures issuing from Rome in 1479, when clergy from Mainz, Trier and Cologne objected to the financial hardship their churches had to bear under papal rule. Eventually this form of protest would be employed by secular rulers as they, too, tried to limit papal power and increase their own.

In 1510, Emperor Maximilian, concerned with the amount of wealth that was being drained from the economy of the empire to Rome, commissioned a catalog of grievances to be presented to the pope. The author of these grievances, humanist and German patriot Jakob Wimpfeling (1415–1528), restated many of the grievances made in the mid-fifteenth century by the chancellor of the Archbishop of Mainz, Martin Mair.[100] Wimpheling understood his task as one of providing the response to Piccolomini that Mair was unable to deliver.

Wimpheling began by revealing his nationalistic tendencies. "Enea, as an Italian and acting from the fear that the copious flow of German money into his country might one day be stopped, sought to refute Martin's charges..." "As a German and on behalf of Germans, ... as a son of the empire and on behalf of the empire, I reply to Enea."[101]

In response to Piccolomini's claim that the German people possessed a great deal of wealth, Wimpheling countered that even if that claim were true, the money was first needed to care for the needs of the German people. He noted: "... how much of it would remain to us after we had taken care of our daily needs, had seen to the maintenance of our churches, cities, streets, and public institutions ... ?"[102]

Wimpheling identified the demands of the curia as "demands coming from Rome dressed in Christian garb but serving Italian interests." The following examples are given: "our compatriots crowd the road to Rome ... pay for papal reservations and dispensations ... appear before papal courts [because] ... their cases have been arbitrarily transferred there ... receive indulgences ... paid dearly for the confirmation of every

---

99. Ibid., 51.

100. See Gebhardt, *Die gravamina*, 83ff. for a comparison of Wimpfeling's and Martin Mair's *gravamina*.

101. Strauss, *Manifestations of Discontent*, 41.

102. Ibid., 42.

bishop and abbot." All this is done in order "to support the innumerable retainers and hangers-on that populate the papal court."[103]

In a laundry-list of grievances, Wimpheling enumerates additional abuses, including:

- Church incomes are given to unworthy men and Italians.
- High offices and lucrative posts are awarded to persons of unproven merit and character.
- Few holders of benefices reside in their churches, for they hold several posts simultaneously.
- Those who hold benefices neglect the care of souls and seek only temporal rewards.
- The divine service is curtailed.
- Striving after pluralities of benefices is encouraged.
- Crooked lawsuits are employed to gather benefices.
- Prelates are deprived of jurisdiction and authority.
- The hierarchical order of the Church is destroyed.[104]

Like Mair, he included in his list of grievances a warning of the popular resentment growing among German subjects as a result of papal abuses of power. "For the sums of money our prelates must send to Rome are taken from the pockets of poor burghers, rural clerics, and impoverished peasants, and many a husband and father cannot nourish his family for the taxes he must pay. Such a reduction of our tribute might well prevent the outbreak of a violent insurrection of our people against the Church."[105]

Finally, Wimpheling called for a reduction in the sale of indulgences claiming "the prolific distribution of indulgences is likely to incline people to immoral lives."[106] Wimpfeling's *Gravamina Germanicae Nationis*, not unlike Luther's "Ninety-Five Theses," were made available to the general public and fueled resentments against the pope.

---

103. Ibid., 43.
104. Ibid., 44.
105. Ibid., 45.
106. Ibid., 47.

Eventually, the term *gravamina* became the rallying cry for anti-papal sentiments among common Germans.

Luther was aware of these *gravamina*, especially the grievances aired at Augsburg in 1518.[107] In his Dedication of the 1519 Lectures on Galatians, Luther lifts up the airing of grievances made by the princes at Augsburg concerning the financial abuses perpetrated against the German people by the Roman Curia:

> Everywhere these impious scoundrels sell themselves as the Roman Church, just as it suits each one, as merely with the lead and wax of the Roman Curia they dupe and drain all Germany. What are they doing with such caricatures of the holy names "pope" and "Roman Church" except that they take us Germans to be mere blockheads, dunces, simpletons, and, as they say, barbarians and beasts, while they even ridicule the incredible patience with which we endure the way they dupe and swindle us? Therefore in such a great muddle of facts and words I return from this great forest of Sylvesters to the city of Augsburg, and meanwhile I shall follow the judgment whereby the princes of Germany at their most recent assembly distinguished in a proper, holy, and majestic way between the Roman Church and the Roman Curia. For how could they have rejected the levies of 10, 5, and 2 percent (that is, the marrow and the sudden devastation once for all of Germany in its entirety) which they knew had been sanctioned in that most sacred (if I may say so) Roman council and had been demanded by such great emissaries of the apostolic see unless finally, though at a late hour, they had become wise and had realized that this was not a decree of the Roman Church but an invention of the Roman Curia?[108]

Thus, the *gravamina* expressed at Augsburg in 1518 most certainly had an influence on his articulation of grievances printed in "To the Christian Nobility of the German Nation." Later in his life, Luther noted that the timing of his own calls for reformation and the *gravamina* presented at the Diet benefited his reform plan.

> The Germans in the meantime, all tired of suffering the pillagings, traffickings, and endless impostures of Roman rascals, awaited with bated breath the outcome of so great a matter, which no one before, neither bishop nor theologian, had dared to touch. In any case that popular breeze favored me, because

---

107. Gebhardt, *Die gravamina*, 126; see also Grimm, *Reformation Era*, 109.
108. LW 27:157.

those practices and "Romanations," with which they had filled and tired the whole earth, were already hateful to all.[109]

Following Luther's publication of "To the Christian Nobility of the German Nation," these *gravamina* became theologically charged and quickly became part of the overall conversation concerning reform of the church. Evidence of this fact is found in the proceedings that took place at the Diet of Worms in 1521. As the newly elected Emperor, Charles V, tried to settle the Luther question. German princes objected by once again pointing to the broad resentments in Germany against the Curia as articulated in a series of *gravamina* presented to the pope throughout the preceding decades. This fact will be explored in greater depth below.

Some Conclusions

It is clear that the cosmology put forward by the pope, and largely accepted by those who stood as subjects to the church, was constructed on a hierarchical axiom which subordinated temporal power to spiritual power. Though this cosmology did not restrain those who held secular power from trying to limit the power of the pope, it provided a conceptual framework for society which gave the pope significant temporal authority.

Yet the authority of the pope was called into question in significant ways during the Middle Ages. Kings challenged the pope; councils challenged the pope; even lower level clerics challenged the pope. These protests against papal authority provided yet another conceptual framework upon which a reform movement could be built. Though the pope was a supreme authority in concept, in reality he had to defend his power from inevitable challenges at almost every period of papal history. For this reason, Luther's challenges to papal authority were not especially unique when seen in light of these historical realities.

The purpose of this study, however, is not to prove that Luther's confrontation with the pope was a unique event. Our intention is to show that in his attack on the power of the papacy, Luther was engaging in an attack on the prevailing political structure of his day. By gaining a better understanding of the cosmology of the Middle Ages, we have

---

109. LW 34:329.

come to recognize that an attack on papal authority was *de facto* an attack on the political structure as it was conceived by the papacy. Yet Luther goes one step further, as we shall see in our next chapter, and redefines the priesthood in an attempt to do much more than simply attack political and ecclesial structures. Through his universal priesthood, he will redefine these structures and the conceptual understanding of temporal authority.

5

Luther's Responses to Claims of Papal Authority in "To the Christian Nobility of the German Nation"

WITH THE PUBLICATION OF "TO THE CHRISTIAN NOBILITY OF THE German Nation" in 1520, Luther restated many of the concerns that had been addressed during prior reform movements. Moreover, Luther connects these grievances to a theological treatise on the nature of baptism and the priesthood. His universal priesthood functioned as a fundamental attack on the medieval cosmology which was the root of papal claims of authority in the temporal sphere. His articulation of the universal priesthood prior to his calls for secular reform had the effect of dismantling all that stood in the way of the success of other reform movements. After tearing down the cosmology of his day, he was then able to consider the best way to rebuild the structures of his day.

Thus, Luther's universal priesthood was not simply another evangelical concept that dealt with the office of ministry. It also served as the means for reordering the concept of temporal authority and the temporal order. Understood in this way, the universal priesthood had a political dimension that must be acknowledged if it is to be fully understood.

Before this assertion can be demonstrated, we must first deal with the historical and social context of Luther's "To the Christian Nobility of the German Nation." Then we will examine the text itself in conversation with the context in which it was written, in order to discern how his theological understanding of the universal priesthood under girds the calls for temporal reform within the document.

Luther and the Papacy

Though the point may be obvious, it is important to note that Luther's understanding of the authority of the pope and the papacy developed as his understanding of the gospel took form. Scott Hendrix has suggested several stages of Luther's understanding of the papacy which are helpful.[1] In order to make clear the development of Luther's understanding of the papacy, I will highlight the stages that Hendrix proposes (with some additional commentary). For the sake of this study, only the stages leading to the publication of "To the Christian Nobility of the German Nation" will be considered.

From the years 1505 to 1515, Luther's attitude towards the papacy has been described as ambivalent.[2] Though Hendrix questions whether or not Luther's words conveyed his true feelings, he reports that near the end of his life Luther recalled his early years as a time when he was an enthusiastic supporter of papal authority over the church and society. "So you will find how much and what important matters I humbly conceded to the pope in my earlier writings, which I later and now hold and execrate as the worst blasphemies and abomination. You will, therefore, sincere reader, ascribe this error, or, as they slander, contradiction to the time and my inexperience. At first I was all alone and certainly very inept and unskilled in conducting such great affairs."[3] Regardless of whether and to what extent Luther was trying to convey a more moderate stance towards the papacy during a time of trouble, there is no reason to believe that much of what Luther said did not in reality reflect his real feelings. In the final analysis of this period, Hendrix surmises that Luther's devotion to the pope was sincere.[4]

The period from October 1517 to June 1518 marked the time during which Luther's positions towards the pope began to take the form of protest.[5] Hendrix is half correct when he asserts that the indulgence controversy in the sixteenth century did not need to lead to a controversy over papal authority. He argues that the real issue at stake was the sacrament of penance. In reality as Hendrix eventually acknowledges,

1. Scott Hendrix, *Luther and the Papacy*.
2. Ibid., 1.
3. LW 34:328.
4. Hendrix, *Luther and the Papacy*, 5.
5. Ibid., 22.

by the fourteenth century formal complaints were being made to the papal curia concerning the extreme financial hardships caused by the selling of indulgences in Germany.[6] Certainly more was at stake to the average person, prince and bishop than the sacrament of penance!

Yet Hendrix is on target when he reminds his reader that all the pent-up frustrations concerning the overwhelming authority and demands of the pope came to a head with the publication of Luther's "Ninety-Five Theses." What Luther called for was not a reappraisal of the legitimacy of the pope, but rather an open dialog concerning the ways in which the church had understood God's forgiveness and the treasury of merits which was so important to the penitential system. Luther's theological questions gave voice to a resentment that reached far beyond the confessional. Luther's call for dialog became a nation's cry of protest.

Events unfolded in a way that Luther had not imagined. He dedicated a copy of his "Ninety- Five Theses" to Pope Leo X and hoped that Leo would see, as Luther himself saw, that the real controversy was not between himself and the Pope. Luther insisted that the real conflict was between him and those who slandered the Pope by selling indulgences in Leo's name. In these explanations, Luther was intent on showing that his argument was not with the Pope, Leo X, but with some understandings of the papacy.

> Although there are in the church men who are most learned as well as most holy, nevertheless it is the tragedy of our age that even such great men are not able to help the church ... Finally, we now have a very good pope, Leo X, whose integrity and learning are a delight to all upright persons. But what can this man who is so worthy of our respect do amidst such confusing circumstances? He is worthy of having become pope in better times, or of having better times during his pontificate. In our day we are only worthy of popes like Julius II, Alexander VI, or some other tyrannous Mezentians as described by the poets. For today even Rome itself laughs at the good popes, indeed Rome most of all. In what part of the Christian world do they ridicule the popes more freely than in that veritable Babylon, Rome?[7]

---

6. See above, section on the *gravamina*.
7. LW 31:155.

Pope Leo X did not see events as Luther saw them. Terms like heretic were being applied to the Augustinian monk. What began as a call for dialog became something altogether different in the following months and years.

Hendrix identifies the specific period from June to December 1518 as one of active resistance on the part of Luther to the demands of the papacy.[8] It was during this period that Luther finally realized that the Pope was personally involved in his case and had chosen to reject Luther's teachings as heretical. With the publication of Sylvester Prierias' "Dialogue Concerning the Power of the Pope," Luther became acutely aware that his challenge against the sale of indulgences had been interpreted as a direct attack on papal authority, which indeed it was, whether Luther admitted it or not. Comments such as,

> I doubt and dispute whether the popes have the power of jurisdiction over purgatory. As much as I have read and perceive up to this moment, I hold fast to the negative position. I am prepared, however, to maintain the affirmative after the church has decided upon it. Meanwhile I speak here concerning power of force, not of rights—the power of working, not of commanding—so that the meaning is this: The pope has absolutely no authority over purgatory, nor does any other bishop. If, however, he does have some authority, he certainly has only the same kind in which his subordinates also share,[9]

could hardly have been interpreted as a wholesale sign of Luther's support of papal authority as it had been traditionally understood!

In August of 1518, the Holy Roman Emperor Maximilian also became involved when he informed Leo that he would be willing to treat Luther as an outlaw heretic if the Pope so desired. By October, Luther was face to face with Cardinal Cajetan who had been instructed by the Pope to secure Luther's recantation of his writings. Failing this goal, Luther was to be handed over to the forces of the Pope to stand trial in Rome. Only the intervention of Luther's elector, Frederick, saved him from an obvious fate. By this time, Luther had given up his hope of convincing the Pope of his intentions and requested an audience with a council of the church.

---

8. Hendrix, *Luther and the Papacy*, 44.
9. LW 31:156.

1519 was a pivotal year for Luther and the development of his understanding of the gospel. He began to consider the papacy the throne of the antichrist and the pope the servant of the antichrist, though he refrained from publishing these thoughts. In addition, during an encounter with Johannes Eck in Leipzig, Luther finally spoke clearly about his reservations concerning papal authority, and in so doing, provided a foretaste of the argument that he would eventually level against papal authority: the priesthood of all believers.

> It is maintained by everyone in the church that in the agony and moment of death every priest is a pope and therefore remits everything for the one who is about to die. And if the priest is absent, certainly the longing of the dying man for the priest is sufficient. For this reason, since the dying man is pardoned for everything which can be pardoned by the pope, the indulgences for the dead seem to confer absolutely nothing, for whatever can be loosed is loosed by death. From this it is likewise evident that the distinction in gradations and laws is to be understood as applying only to the living and those who are in good health. Therefore indulgences evidently apply only to criminals and to the living who are healthy and strong, who have no hindrances and who have no desire to mend their ways. If I am wrong in this, let him correct me, whoever is able and knows.[10]

In the year 1520, what had been resistance to the pope's decrees and power had turned into open opposition. Though Luther did not have it in mind to openly revolt against the papacy,[11] he did begin to challenge the ontological groundwork of the papacy as he began to publish his understanding of the pope as the antichrist.

> See how different Christ is from his successors, although they all would wish to be his vicars. I fear that most of them have been too literally his vicars. A man is a vicar only when his superior is absent. If the pope rules, while Christ is absent and does not dwell in his heart, what else is he but a vicar of Christ? What is the church under such a vicar but a mass of people without Christ? Indeed, what is such a vicar but an antichrist and an idol? How much more properly did the apostles call them-

---

10. LW 31:122.
11. Hendrix, *Luther and the Papacy*, 97.

selves servants of the present Christ and not vicars of an absent Christ?[12]

Additionally, at this time, Luther shifted his attention to a different audience. Rather than attempt to change the church from within the clerical hierarchy, he started to address his writings to the laity; a move that would also lead him to challenge the foundations of the papal office.

On another front, during the early months of 1520, Luther read Lorenzo Valla's work rejecting the "Donation of Constantine" on the grounds that it was an eighth-century forgery. This fueled Luther's belief that the pope had no authority to act as a temporal ruler and could be opposed if he oppressed the lives and consciences of the German people, a point that will be explored in more detail below. Into this context, Luther gave birth to his political manifesto which would challenge the authority of the pope and lead him to most clearly articulate one of his most famous doctrines: the priesthood of all believers. Monk and Pope had set their faces against one another. Luther published his attacks, and the Pope issued a threat of excommunication. By the end of 1520, Luther responded to the Pope's claim of authority over his life and teaching by burning the papal bull which threatened his life and soul.

Luther's "To The Christian Nobility of the German Nation" in Context

In a letter written to his friend and comrade Spalatin in the beginning of June 1520, Luther writes, "It is in my mind to put out a public writing to Charles and the whole German nobility against the tyranny and wickedness of the Roman curia."[13]

Luther was right to be confident in his decision to write such a treatise. He had been assured that he would receive protection if his words against the pope would bring about a threat to his security. Silvester von Schaumburg pledged one hundred knights to serve as Luther's personal protectors. Humanists Ulrich von Hutten and Franz von Sickingen also offered their support. Sickingen offered the protection of his castle at Ebernburg. Hutten attempted to enlist Luther as an ally in his "national

12. LW 31:341.
13. Martin Luther, *D. Martin Luthers* Werke, Br, 2, 120. Hereafter cited as WA. "Est animus publicam schedam edere ad Carolum & totius germanie nobilitatem aduersus Ro[manae] Curie tyrannidem & nequitiam."

revolutionary movement against Rome."[14] In fact, it has been argued by some that these prominent figures actually influenced Luther's thinking to such an extent that Luther had simply taken upon himself their war against papal abuses. Yet, the editor of the *Weimar Ausgabe* edition of "To the Christian Nobility of the German Nation" asserts that Luther had independently come to his own understanding of the problem of the papacy and had developed his program on his own.[15]

Luther was aware of the intentions of Hutten and his group of humanist patriots. Speaking of Hutten, Luther declared: "You can see what Hutten has in mind. I do not want the gospel to be contested by force and the shedding of blood . . . Through the Word the world was overcome, through the Word the church was maintained, and through the Word she will again be restored."[16] Luther was right to be concerned about Hutten's desire for German strength to be shown through armed conflict. Hutten's call for the renewal of German power was obvious when he encouraged his leaders to make war with the Turks. "Carry on war, and let us rise, immediately the old glory will flourish, immediately Germany will again become a bright power . . ."[17] Fearing that Hutten's desire was to restore the glories of Germany through force of arms, be it against the Turk or the pope, Luther relied on the only protection he ever needed: the grace of God and the influence of his elector.

Though Hutten is most often cited as an influence on Luther's political treatise, his was certainly not the only voice whispering in Luther's ear during the period in which he considered and wrote his manifesto. For instance, after Luther had decided to request from the Emperor a general council in order to bring about the needed reforms of the church, a number of Saxon lawyers met with the faculty of the University of Wittenberg to discuss the exact problems to be addressed, a meeting which certainly helped those present, including Philip Melanchthon, to identify specific abuses which such a council would address.[18]

As to the question concerning how Luther, who only experienced Rome as a young monk in 1510–1511, had such insight into the work-

14. Grimm, *The Reformation Era*, 107.
15. WA 6: 381ff.
16. LW 32:XII. WA, Br 2, 249.
17. Von Hutten, *Ulrichs von Hutten Schriften*, 110.
18. Schwiebert, *Luther and His Times*, 466.

ings of the city nearly a decade after his infamous trip, Schwiebert suggests that his information came from reports made by Johann von der Wieck, who had gathered a wealth of information on the conditions in the holy city and passed the information on to Luther. These reports were augmented by Luther's correspondence with a member of the Saxon court, Hans von Taubenheim.[19]

Whatever the reasons behind Luther's decision to write his now famous address to the Christian nobility, it is clear from the text that Luther was aware of the history of doctrine that was utilized by the church to enforce adherence to papal authority in secular matters, especially in—but not limited to—such documents as the "Donation of Constantine" and *Unam Sanctam*. Additionally, he was aware of, and in fact already utilized, a present set of protests which had become a rallying cry for the German people against the abuses of the pope as they were to be found in the traditions of the *gravamina*. What remains to be explored is how each of these factors were either attacked or utilized by Luther in "To the Christian Nobility of the German Nation."

Considering the context of his day and the influences of his context, we are now ready to begin examining how these contexts overtly influenced Luther's "To the Christian Nobility of the German Nation" and his overall desire to reform both the political and spiritual estates through his doctrine of the priesthood of all believers.

At two points in his work, Luther indicates why he has set out to write this treatise. The first comes in his greeting to Nicholas von Amsdorf, where Luther reveals that "I am carrying out our intention to put together a few points on the matter of the reform of the Christian estate, to be laid before the Christian nobility of the German nation, in the hope that God may help his church through the laity..."[20]

In his opening remarks to his intended audience, the emperor and the Christian nobility of the German nation, Luther once again lifts up the cause of the German people: "All the estates of Christendom, particularly in Germany, are now oppressed by distress and affliction, and this has stirred not only me but everybody else to cry out time and time again and to pray for help. It has even compelled me now at this time to cry aloud that God may inspire someone with his Spirit to lend a help-

---

19. Ibid., 467.
20. LW 44:123.

ing hand to this distressed and wretched nation."[21] Thus, Luther's cause is the cause of the German nation. This is much more than a theological treatise, but a political document which has as its main aim the betterment of German society.

Luther says as much when he describes the papal sapping of German resources through annates and benefices as "the heart of the matter."[22] Luther has determined to articulate his evangelical theology in order to reform both the church and the state.

The Text

The First Wall

Fully understanding the doctrines which asserted papal authority over temporal and sacred estates, Luther recognized that the papacy had no incentive to reform itself. He hoped that the true reform of the church would now be undertaken not from within the church hierarchy, but rather from within the laity, "since the clergy, to whom this task more properly belongs, have grown quite indifferent."[23]

In order to make his point, Luther expressed his concern that three walls had been built by Rome to protect it against reform.

The first wall was the doctrine that temporal powers are subject to spiritual power. Luther was aware of the tradition surrounding the "Donation," and was convinced by the arguments against its authenticity leveled by Valla and Hutten.

> That impossible lie, the *Donation of Constantine*, . . . must have been some special plague from God that so many intelligent people have let themselves be talked into accepting such lies. They are so crude and clumsy that I should imagine any drunken peasant could lie more adroitly and skillfully. How can a man rule and at the same time preach, pray, study, and care for the poor? Yet these are the duties which most properly and peculiarly belong to the pope, and they were so earnestly imposed by Christ that he even forbade his disciples to take cloak or money with them [Matt. 10:9–10]. Christ commanded this because it is almost impossible for anybody to fulfill these duties if they

21. LW 44:124.
22. LW 44:143.
23. LW 44:123.

have to look after one single household. Yet the pope would rule an empire and still remain pope. This is what those rogues have thought up who, under the cover of the pope's name, would like to be lords of the world and would gladly restore the Roman Empire to its former state through the pope and in the name of Christ.[24]

His response to this wall, constructed on the foundation of an "impossible lie" and papal *bullae* such as *Unam Sanctam*, was to declare that "all Christians are truly of the spiritual estate."[25] Luther found points of agreement with the medieval understanding that all Christendom was united as the one body of Christ. Yet Luther veers away from the conclusions drawn from the accepted interpretation of this understanding of the church and society. Where the medieval popes understood the need for the one body to be controlled by a special portion of the body, Luther concluded that every part of the body had the right and obligation to come to the aid of the other members. Luther allowed for no distinction in the matter of estate. Only in office was Luther willing to acknowledge a degree of differentiation. Christ does not have two different bodies, one temporal, the other spiritual. There is but one Head and one body. As he unfolded his argument, the political dimensions of his theology of the priesthood of all believers was unmistakable. "We are all consecrated priests through baptism,"[26] he asserted. Thus,

> since those who exercise secular authority have been baptized with the same baptism, and have the same faith and the same gospel as the rest of us, we must admit that they are priests and bishops and we must regard their office as one which has a proper and useful place in the Christian community ... It follows from this argument that there is no true, basic difference between laymen and priests, princes and bishops, between religious and secular, except for the sake of office and work, but not for the sake of status.[27]

This claim impacts how the body of Christ and the hierocratic axiom is fundamentally understood.

---

24. LW 44:166.
25. LW 44:127.
26. LW 44:127.
27. LW 44:129.

> Consider for a moment how Christian is the decree which says that the temporal power is not above the "spiritual estate" and has no right to punish it. That is as much as to say that the hand shall not help the eye when it suffers pain. Is it not unnatural, not to mention un-Christian, that one member does not help another and prevent its destruction? In fact, the more honorable the member, the more the others ought to help. I say therefore that since the temporal power is ordained of God to punish the wicked and protect the good, it should be left free to perform its office in the whole body of Christendom without restriction and without respect to persons, whether it affects pope, bishops, priests, monks, nuns, or anyone else.[28]

For Luther, this is all that is needed to destroy the first wall. We recall the ancient understanding of the nature of spiritual and temporal power, as first articulated by Leo I and Gelasius I. Leo believed that in order for the mystical body of Christ to have any concrete presence it must be rooted in the spiritual elements of the Christian faith which is made manifest in the Church. Thus the body is only properly directed by the spiritual estate and those who hold spiritual offices.

Gelasius understood the nature of power as existing in degrees, but emanating from the primary authority (*principitus*) which was the possession of the pope. The consecrated priests exercised authority (*auctoritas*) while the temporal authorities, including royal powers, were limited to exercising power (*potestas*) in the name of the principle authority. The consecrated priesthood defined the nature of power in the medieval world. However, if all members of the body are equally priests, each member has the right and authority to intervene when the body as a whole is in need. Here Luther's understanding of estate (*Stand*) and office (*Amt*) become critical. The only thing that separates one Christian from another within the communion of saints is the office each holds within the body. All Christians are of the same estate by nature of baptism. The modern reader recognizes in these passages more than the destruction of the first wall of papal protection. If one remembers Ullmann's claim that medieval society was defined by the separation of lay and cleric, a modern reader can recognize that Luther is now attacking the very foundations of medieval cosmology by placing every baptized Christian in the estate formerly reserved for the priests. Any notion of papal *plentitudo potestas* is completely rejected.

28. LW 44:130.

What remains to be seen is if Luther wished to replace that cosmology with another.

Luther and the Orders of Creation: An Excursus

The cosmology that Luther attacked was rooted in an understanding that the will of God for creation was made manifest in an institution. Though Luther does not immediately make the claim in "To the Christian Nobility of the German Nation" that he was articulating a new cosmology, his treatise does seem to hint at what scholars have come to call his "orders of creation." For Luther, cosmology is not made manifest in institutions, but rather is to be understood as that which God calls into being through his Word of institution.[29]

According to Oswald Bayer, "Language gives nature a constitution, demarcates characteristics and certainty, imposes order upon courses of action, and thus makes human life possible as a life in the perspectives of memory and hope. It was this issue which Martin Luther addressed with his doctrine of three orders (*Dreiständelehre*)."[30]

Luther's three orders of creation provide us with his exegetical method for understanding the biblical narrative of primordial times and the emergence of the created order, sin and the ordering of the social world. Because Luther held that the orders of creation were of fundamental importance he upheld the doctrine as the "first principle of scriptural exegesis."[31]

In his 1528 treatise "Confession Concerning Christ's Supper," Luther makes reference to what he calls "holy orders and true religious institutions established by God."[32] The three holy orders are the church, the estate of marriage and the civil government. "For these three religious institutions or orders are found in God's Word and commandment."[33] Luther is able to conclude that even princes, lords, civil officers and state officials are "engaged in pure holiness and leading a holy life before God."[34] These "orders of creation" are Luther's attempt at arriving at

29. Bayer, "Nature and Institution," 134.
30. Ibid., 126.
31. Ibid., 127.
32. LW 37:364.
33. LW 37:365.
34. LW 37:365.

a biblical narrative about the creation and how this narrative informs contemporary situations.[35]

Luther follows these statements with the claim that what was ordered by God in creation serves the purpose of exercising Christian love. Certainly Luther is careful to separate the acts of love with the gift of justification, but he does root these acts, and the institutions mentioned which are tasked with carrying out acts of love, in his conception of God's will for all creation. This is a fundamentally ethical and existential cosmology, which serves to underscore the work of all Christians along the lines of his articulation of the universal priesthood in "To the Christian Nobility of the German Nation."

Bayer contends that for Luther, "Every human being belongs ... to the ecclesial order of creation ... Inserted into this basic order of the church ... is the creation of the household, or of the economy ... Luther did not recognize the third order ... as an order of creation, seeing it rather merely as an expedient made necessary only by the fall."[36]

Bayer finds a way of placing a limit on Luther's political thinking by presuming—without reference to Luther himself—that Luther was unable to afford the civil government the same standing as the church and the household. However, one can argue from Luther's own writings that Luther placed all the orders under the heading of spiritual orders of God. What makes them spiritual is that they have been instituted by God's Word, as Bayer himself asserts.[37]

Bayer references Luther's *Smalcald Articles* and highlights Luther's belief that the church has been enlightened by God to understand the connection between the pure Word of God, the right use of the sacraments and the proper understanding of the various callings in life. In this way Luther raises the importance of the orders of creation to the level of Word and sacrament.

Luther's use of the three orders avoids the possible conclusion that one can easily separate church from state. Instead, his three orders highlight the reality that "the spiritual is not only inwardly, but also outwardly, temporal. The temporal, in turn, is spiritual, insofar as it is the governance of *God* on earth."[38]

---

35. Bayer, "Nature and Institution," 127.
36. Ibid., 128.
37. Ibid., 134.
38. Ibid., 130.

This thinking is a radical departure from the early Luther who had not yet begun to attack medieval cosmology manifest in the institutions of the church. As an Augustinian monk, Luther had come to think of the natural order in terms of the demand for escape from the world. We recall that by the late medieval period, it was assumed that temporal matters had no independent value and were defined only in their relation to the spiritual realm.[39] One could argue, based on the "Heidelberg Disputation" (1518) that for Luther, the world and nature had no inherent dignity or positive spiritual weight. However, Luther's new cosmology rooted in the reality of a world instituted by God's own command and Word, was intensely aware of the world in the positive sense. From 1520 on, one finds in Luther's writings an "impressive affirmation of all wordly and natural things."[40] The spiritual significance of all things worldly was revealed to him.[41] His new understanding of the Word and sacraments indicated Luther's understanding of a worldly mediation of the spiritual world, and a spiritual significance to all things worldly. This new thinking was especially prevalent in Luther's understanding of marriage, parenthood and worldly government.[42]

What is of significant value to this work is the connection between Luther's understanding of the created order and the sacrament of baptism. The first evidence of Luther's positive understanding of the temporal world, in opposition to the medieval cosmology, is to be found in Luther's 1519 "The Holy and Blessed Sacrament of Baptism." Bayer highlights the following words written by Luther: "[God] has instituted many estates in life in which [people] are to learn to exercise themselves and to suffer. To some he has commanded the estate of matrimony, to others the estate of clergy, to others the estate of temporal rule, and to all [God] has commanded that they shall toil and labor to kill the flesh and accustom it to death."[43]

In his 1520 treatise "The Freedom of a Christian," Luther highlights the necessity of living a spiritual life which is at the same time oriented towards the love of neighbor expressed in concrete acts. People are not simply to live for themselves, but for all people. For this reason the body

39. See above, chapter 4.
40. Bayer, "Nature and Institution," 133.
41. Ibid., 134.
42. Ibid.
43. Ibid., quoting LW 35:39.

must be subjected, not in order to escape the world, but rather in order to serve the world.[44]

However, Bayer does not make reference to Luther's "To the Christian Nobility of the German Nation." It remains a mystery why he decides to overlook the treatise that seems to best articulate the connection between the orders of creation, and indeed most potently suggests how this new cosmology may indeed lead to shifts in how the world is structured.

The Second Wall

In "To the Christian Nobility of the German Nation," Luther continued his attack on the papacy by attacking the second wall. According to Luther, the Romanists had not only usurped temporal authority, but had also claimed the right to interpret scripture, thereby furthering the notion that the pope was infallible in matters of faith,[45] a claim made by both Alveld and Prierias.[46]

The pope and his supporters claimed to be the only masters of the faith. Luther charged that they have yet to prove that they have learned a single thing from scripture. Worse yet is the claim that the pope cannot err in matters of faith. In his treatise against Luther's "Ninety-Five Theses," Prierias claimed "The supreme pontiff cannot err when giving a decision as a pontiff, i.e., when speaking officially" and "Even though the pope as an individual can do wrong and hold a wrong faith, nevertheless as pope he cannot give a wrong decision."[47]

Though the concept of papal infallibility was not an official teaching of the church during the Middle Ages, the doctrine of papal authority virtually established papal infallibility. For example, ecumenical councils could not be called—nor could their conclusions be officially recognized—without the authority of the pope (a matter to be dealt with specifically in Luther's attack on the third wall). However, such noted theologians as William of Ockham and Pierre d'Ailly, as we have noted above, had formally attacked the notion that the pope cannot err.

---

44. LW 31:364.
45. LW 44:133.
46. Schwiebert, *Luther and His Times*, 470.
47. LW 44:133 n. 31.

Both thinkers argued that only the mystical body of Christ can claim to be without error. The official head of the body, the pope, can err.

Again Luther relied on the common authority of all the baptized and asserted that "if we are all priests, as was said above, and all have one faith, one gospel, one sacrament, why should we not also have the power to test and judge what is right or wrong in matters of faith?" In light of such awareness, "We ought to become bold and free."[48] Where, Luther demanded, was evidence for this position from scripture? Certainly supporters of papal infallibility had produced scriptural evidence for the claim. Most prominent are Matthew 16:18 (granting of the keys to Peter), Luke 22:31–32 (prayer of Christ for the protection of Peter), John 21:15–17 (three-fold command to feed the sheep). Yet Luther was having none of it. "Since these Romanists think the Holy Spirit never leaves them, no matter how ignorant and wicked they are, they become bold and decree only what they want. And if what they claim were true, why have Holy Scripture at all? Of what use is scripture? Let us burn the Holy Scripture and be satisfied with the unlearned gentlemen at Rome who possess the Holy Spirit!"[49]

Luther dispensed with the claim that Jesus gives Peter the keys by arguing "the keys were not given to Peter alone but to the whole community. Further, the keys were not ordained for doctrine or government, but only for the binding of sin."[50] As for Christ's prayer for the protection of Peter, Luther casually claims that this prayer cannot be applied to the pope because "the majority of popes have been without faith." However, Luther does also rely on the foundational argument that "it is not only for Peter that Christ prayed, but also for all apostles and Christians..."[51]

In addition to Luther's attack on papal interpretations of key scripture, he also contends that to give all authority in matters of faith to the pope would be a negation of the creed. "Again, if the article, 'I believe in one holy Christian church,' is correct, then the pope cannot be the only one who is right. Otherwise, we would have to confess, 'I believe in the pope at Rome.'"[52]

48. LW 44:135.
49. LW 44:134.
50. LW 44:134.
51. LW 44:135.
52. LW 44:135.

In the final analysis, each Christian is compelled to put forward the cause of faith above all things. In the face of these great errors, every Christian must denounce the false teachings of the papacy in regards to the pope's right to be the sole interpreter of matters of the faith.

The Third Wall

At this point Luther finally attacked the third wall: only the pope may call a council. According to Luther, this "wall falls of itself when the first two are down."[53] In this portion of his argument, we are reminded of the Investiture Controversy. It was Gregory VII in his *Dictatus* who had asserted that no council was authoritative unless it has the official sanctioning of the pope.[54] Prierias had defended papal authority on this point as well when he wrote, "when there is one undisputed pontiff, it belongs to him alone to call a council . . . the decrees of the council neither bind nor hold unless they are confirmed by the authority of the pope."[55] Yet these positions had been attacked by some of the most prominent theologians of the fourteenth and fifteenth centuries during the conciliar movement.

In the Acts of the Apostles, it is not Peter who calls the Apostolic Council. The council is called by the apostles and elders of the church. As to who should call a council to reform the church, Luther asserts: "No one can do this so well as the temporal authorities, especially since they are fellow-Christians, fellow priests, fellow-members of the spiritual estate, fellow-lords over all things." How does Luther justify such a claim? He articulates the doctrine of the universal priesthood. He asserts that temporal authorities must utilize the power of their offices. Indeed, this is God's will. The offices given to those who hold temporal power were given to them by God to be utilized for the sake of the gospel.[56]

For Luther this was perfectly in keeping with the traditions of the church. "Even the Council of Nicaea, the most famous of all councils, was neither called nor confirmed by the bishop of Rome, but by the

---

53. LW 44:136.
54. Schwiebert, *Luther and His Times*, 471.
55. LW 44:136 n. 136.
56. LW 44:137.

emperor Constantine. Many other emperors after him have done the same, and yet these councils were the most Christian of all."[57]

Luther could also rely on the witness of the Paris theologians. Theologians at the University of Paris, during the period of the reform councils (1409-1450), had determined that the claim of the pope to have authority over councils was not in keeping with the practices of the early church.[58]

No person, according to Luther, has the authority to injure the church or her members. The purpose of authority given by God to the church is to promote good. When a leader of the church injures the church, that leader is no longer in authority. "Therefore, if the pope were to use his authority to prevent the calling of a free council, thereby preventing the improvement of the church, we should have regard neither for him nor for his authority."[59] The punishment for such a pope would be the punishment given to anyone who would do violence to the ministry of the church. He should be excommunicated.

If some sort of negative miracle should be done against the temporal rulers on the pope's behalf, such as an outbreak of plague, this should not be interpreted as divine punishment for temporal hubris, as had been claimed in the past. Rather, this should be interpreted as the work of the devil intended to destroy the faith of true believers.[60] Therefore, temporal rules should have no fear when confronting those popes who act in ways contrary to the evangelical doctrine. As Luther will spell out in the pages that follow, it will be up to the temporal authorities, and them alone, to take back the authority given to them by God to rule the world and protect and reform the church by virtue of their divine calling and priesthood.

This position is also in keeping with the idea put forward by Francesco Zabaralla during the conciliar movement, who claimed that if the College of Cardinals fails to exercise its authority in a time of crisis, the authority to call a council falls to the emperor as the representative of the people.[61]

---

57. LW 44:137.
58. Schwiebert, *Luther and His Times*, 471.
59. LW 44:138.
60. LW 44:138.
61. Spinka, *John Hus*, 20. See above, "conciliar movement," chapter 4.

Luther's attack on the power of the pope contained many elements that had been present in earlier reform movements. However, as Luther considered the papacy, he did so from the standpoint of one who no longer accepted the cosmology of the day. Luther refused to accept the absorption of the temporal into the spiritual as a way of limiting temporal authority. He does this by acknowledging the unified body of Christ and the universal church. However, he rejects the notion of separate estates within the body. If the temporal is to be united with the spiritual, neither shall claim dominance over the other using the concept of estate. Rather, distinctions will be based on the different functions within the same body.

Based on this new vision of the body of Christ and its members, all of whom are priests and thus share the same estate, Luther is now ready to announce his reform program. He operates from the assumption that temporal authorities are not to beg for the right to exercise their office. Rather, by divine calling, he expects them to carryout their office as priests and servants. In this way, Luther's reform program is fundamentally different than the reform programs that had been undertaken during the medieval period.

Luther's Demands for Reform: The Heart of the Matter

Following a description of the walls which the papacy used to protect itself from reform and Luther's attempt to justify their destruction, he proceeded to construct his plan for how church and emperor might rebuild a more appropriate structure to protect the Christian church from the power of the pope. It must be noted that by rebuilding a more appropriate structure to protect the church, he is also reconstructing the structures of temporal power.

His proposals for reform of the church and society were hardly original. Indeed, he essentially addressed the issues that had been brought before the pope for reform for years in the *gravamina*. Many of his reform proposals had also been addressed at the Council of Constance, especially those dealing with the collection of papal taxes.

To begin, Luther called for the matters needing reform to be brought to a council. If no council deals properly with the issues at stake, "let ordinary people and the temporal authorities do it."[62]

62. LW 44:139.

In keeping with the *gravamina*, Luther attacked the ostentation of the papacy, not simply because it was an affront to Christian values of moderation, but mainly because the pomposity of the curia was being paid for by draining funds from Germany. The reader is reminded that the same critique of the papacy was leveled by William of Ockham and others in the fifteenth century. Luther is unwilling to extend to the pope, or any other servant of the church, the wealth, power or status of a royal personage. "The pope's office should be nothing else but to weep and pray for Christendom and set an example of utter humility." This office would not include temporal power. "The Romanists say [the pope] is a lord of the earth. That is a lie! For Christ, whose vicar and vicegerent he claims to be, said to Pilate 'My Kingdom is not of this world.'"[63]

In addition, Luther attacked the College of Cardinals who, according to Luther, had sucked Italy dry and was now intent on feeding on the German economy in order to survive.[64] Indeed, the size of the Cardinals' courts in Rome alone was quite significant. In the mid-sixteenth century the Cardinal's court in that one city, along with the papal household, accounted for seven percent of the adult population in Rome.[65]

For Luther, these abuses of the German people, the draining of funds to pay for the largesse of the church in Rome, were the "heart of the matter." He worried that the princes and nobles, cities and endowments, land and people were growing poor only to support unchristian behavior which supported the hierarchy of the church. Specifically he attacked annates and benefices. Annates were the first year's income owed through the revenue acquired by the holder of a benefice, of this more will be written below. A benefice was defined by canon law as "a juridical entity established or erected in perpetuity by competent ecclesiastical authority, consisting of a sacred office and the right to receive the revenues connected with the office."[66] A benefice was essentially a license granted to a cleric to receive revenues based on his holding an ecclesiastical office. Additionally, he questioned the necessity of the repeated taxations that were supposedly used to make war with the Turks

---

63. LW 44:140.
64. LW 44:141.
65. Fragnito, "Cardinals' Courts," 26.
66. Quoted in Sweet, "Papal Privilege," 602.

but were instead lining the pockets of church officials.[67] As we examine each of Luther's proposals, the consistent refrain is that papal taxes must be curbed if not outright abolished.

Luther now comes to the defense of his German people. "The 'drunken Germans' are not supposed to understand what the Romanists are up to until there is not a bishopric, a monastery, a living, a benefice, not a red cent left." He continues by analyzing how the Germans will be dispossessed of their wealth and resources by the church. "It works like this: they skim the cream off the bishoprics, monasteries, and benefices and because they do not yet venture to put them all to shameful use, as they have done in Italy, they in the meantime practice their holy cunning and couple together ten or twenty prelacies . . . In this way one thousand or ten thousand gulden may be collected, so that a cardinal could live like a wealthy monarch in Rome."[68]

In order to halt these abuses, Luther called upon the princes to begin assuming the responsibility of ruling over their subjects in spiritual and temporal matters, thus sparing them from further abuses.[69]

In addition to those abuses already enumerated, Luther was merciless in attacking such practices as taking the property of those who die in Rome or on pilgrimage to Rome. During the late Middle Ages, a tax called "the spoils" claimed all moveable property belonging to deceased clerics. The earliest spoils taken by the papacy were the possessions and wealth of clergy who died *en route* to Rome. This custom dates back to the late thirteenth century. Pope John XXII (1316–1334) claimed the right to collect all spoils of clergy on pilgrimage who died outside Rome. Urban V issued the first general reservation claiming the right of the pope to inherit all spoils of clerics in 1362. Thus, the seizure of clerical wealth, in particular those who traveled to Rome on pilgrimage, was a source of revenue for the curia.[70]

Luther also attacked the practice of assuming the wealth of all those who enter into service in the papal household, false disputes that extorted money from local clergy in order to protect their benefices, the origination of bishoprics in Rome which kept bishops from reforming the church in their own lands, the installation of coadjucators from

---

67. LW 44:143.
68. LW 44:141.
69. LW 44:144–45.
70. Stump, "The Reform of Papal Taxation," 79.

Rome to assume the role of bishops who have grown infirm,[71] the rejection of *incompatabilia*—the understanding that multiple church offices cannot be held by a single person-[72] and the selling of indulgences.[73]

In order to see an end to these abuses, Luther laid out twenty-six proposals for the reform of the church (and a final proposal which dealt with the reform of secular matters making a total of twenty-seven proposals). For Luther, the necessary reforms should be carried out "either by the temporal authority or by a general council."[74]

Reform Proposals

The first task is for the authorities to forbid the payments of annates to Rome.[75] Each person given a benefice[76] had to pay either annates or services. These twin taxes together provided the largest source of papal income.[77] Services were taxes paid by higher ranking ecclesiastical officials such as bishops and abbots, and annates were paid on lesser benefices.[78] In the late medieval period, benefice taxes were an extremely important source of income for the papacy. They were collected based on the pope's right to dispose of ecclesiastical benefices or dignities which were subject to papal taxation. The income for these taxes was then divided up between the pope and the College of Cardinals.[79] These taxes were not established by papal bull, but were established by longstanding customs. The first year of a benefice was traditionally reserved for the pope.[80] The term annate comes from the word *annata*, and referred to a period of time, a year. In the later half of the fourteenth century, the term was applied to the tax itself. However, by the time of the reform councils the term came to refer to any funds paid to the pope on the receipt of an ecclesial benefice or dignity. Annates were similar to another

71. LW 44:146–49.
72. LW 44:150.
73. LW 44:155.
74. LW 44:156.
75. LW 44:156.
76. See above, n.200. [X-ref]
77. Stump, "Reform of Papal Taxation," 84.
78. Ibid.
79. Lunt, "Financial System," 283.
80. Ibid., 287.

tax, the *fructus medii temporis* or *vacantes*. These were incomes from benefices accrued during the intervening period between occupancies of ecclesiastical benefices and also went to the pope.[81] The importance of annates for the funding of the papal curia cannot be overstated as annates provided some of the largest portions of papal income.[82]

Second, the authorities should forbid the pope from taking funds through various devices from Germany and giving them to foreigners in Rome. "For this reason the Christian nobility should set itself against the pope as against a common enemy and destroyer of Christendom for the salvation of the poor souls who perish because of this tyranny."[83] We will encounter this theme throughout Luther's reform program. Luther's desire is to localize control over funds and positions of power.

Third, Luther demanded that an imperial law be issued that would allow only German bishops or the archbishop to confirm German bishops, as stipulated in the Council of Nicaea.[84] This would guarantee the right of local leaders to choose for themselves those who would serve in their homeland. This would be in keeping with Luther's desire for localization of control over resources and positions of power.

Maintaining this theme, Luther's fourth reform was an insistence that no temporal matter should be referred to Rome. Instead, all temporal issues should be handled by local temporal authorities. "The temporal authorities, therefore, should not permit sentences of excommunication and exile to be passed where faith and morality are not involved. Spiritual authorities should rule over matters which are spiritual; this is just a matter of common sense. But spiritual matters are not money or material things; they are faith and good works."[85]

Fifth, benefices should not be seized by the papacy.[86]

Sixth, reserved cases, or cases which must be reserved for the pope in order for absolution to be administered, must be abolished, thus giving local priests the right to remit all sins without the intervention of Rome.[87] Abolishing the pope's prerogative to settle conflicts in Rome

---

81. Lunt, "Financial System," 288.
82. Stump, "Reform of Papal Taxation," 84.
83. LW 44: 158.
84. LW 44: 158. See note 111.
85. LW 44:160.
86. LW 44: 161.
87. LW 44: 162.

had political consequences. It was not uncommon for the pope to determine the final results of disputed elections by claiming that these elections were reserved cases to be settled only by the pope. This limited the power of local authorities to fill vacant political and ecclesiastical offices. By the thirteenth century this practice was quite common. One example of this papal prerogative can be found in the disputed election of an archbishop in the see of Trier in 1430. The Archbishop of Trier also served as an elector of the empire. The office of Archbishop was an elected office and typically the local cathedral chapter elected the next Archbishop and thus also elected an elector. Following the death of Archbishop Otto of Ziegenhain, on February 13, 1430, the election of a new archbishop became contested and the pope was called upon to choose between the two parties who were being considered for the posts of Archbishop and elector. Pope Martin V, rather than choosing between the two chose his own candidate and thus was able to control the election.[88] Used in this way, reserved cases provided the pope with an excuse to determine the outcome of important elections.

Seventh, the pope must reduce the size of the Roman curia, and the papal household should be supported by the pope himself.[89] To put this reform proposal in perspective, there were seven hundred members of the papal court in 1526,[90] all of whom were supported through various papal taxes.

Eighth, the oath of loyalty taken by bishops to the pope must be abolished and the practice of investiture was to be done away with. For Luther, the right to invest church leaders with temporal powers belonged rightly and only to emperor and kings.[91] Recalling the Investiture controversy and the impact the conflict had on the medieval cosmology, this reform proposal would aid Luther in his desire to empower the temporal authorities. It was the Investiture controversy which solidified the incorporation of the natural world into the supernatural world and justified the pope's claim that only the "functionally qualified" were justified in claiming to possess authority to rule. Through his doctrine of the universal priesthood, Luther redefined the terms of what consti-

---

88. Morimichi Watanabe, "The Episcopal Election," 307–8.
89. LW 44: 163.
90. Fragnito, "Cardinals' Courts," 26 n. 1.
91. LW 44:164

tuted functional qualification. This reform proposal has a direct impact on the ninth reform proposal.

Luther's ninth suggestion for reform goes directly to the point of this case study. The pope is to have no authority over the emperor, nor should the emperor be forced to participate in acts that subordinate him to the pope such as kissing his feet or holding his stirrup.

> This most extreme, arrogant, and wanton presumption of the pope has been devised by the devil, who under cover of this intends to usher in the Antichrist and raise the pope above God, as many are now doing and even have already done. It is not proper for the pope to exalt himself above the temporal authorities, except in spiritual offices such as preaching and giving absolution. In other matters the pope is subject to the crown, as Paul and Peter teach in Romans 13[:1–7] and I Peter 2[:13], and as I have explained above.[92]

Nor is the pope to be considered the rightful heir to the empire in the case of imperial vacancies. All the stipulations of the "Donation of Constantine" are to be considered lies and completely disregarded.[93]

Tenth, the pope should make no claim to the kingdom of Naples and Sicily, nor should the emperor allow the pope any authority in these lands. The claim that the pope ruled these lands went back to the eleventh century and was a cause of some disturbance even in Luther's time.[94] Additionally, the pope was to have no temporal authority in any of the areas in which he was currently assuming control including Bologna, Imola, Ravenna, the territories in March of Ancona, and Romagna.[95] The insistence that the pope claim no temporal authority over these regions was also an attack on a source of papal income through taxation. The revenue the pope received due to his temporal sovereignty had once been the source of the main financial support of the papacy.[96]

This revenue, which the pope received from the territory over which he claimed temporal sovereignty, was the kind ordinarily received by the landlord in the medieval period. These revenues would have included taxes such as returns from the land cultivated under di-

---

92. LW 44:165.
93. LW 44:166.
94. LW 44:166.
95. LW 44:167.
96. Lunt, "The Financial System," 273.

rect management, fees for pasturage, mills and fishing rights. The arrival of a new rector was also an occasion for a tax to be collected from a city, castle and lord. The pope could also rely on indirect taxes such as tolls and customs.[97]

Eleventh, all special honors, such as the kissing of the pope's feet and his being carried aloft, must end.[98] These honors made the pope appear to be a ruler rather than a servant, a king rather than a priest.

The twelfth proposal called for the abolition of pilgrimages to Rome. If Christians wish to go on pilgrimage, the journey should be for the sake of curiosity alone.[99]

Thirteenth, mendicant houses must be abolished and the divisions in current orders must be abolished.[100] This reform proposal also had financial implications for the church. Dating back to the ninth century, monastic orders commonly placed themselves under the protection of the pope. These monasteries gave their possessions to the pope; in return the pope retained absolute ownership of the property controlled by the monasteries. The purpose of such an agreement was to protect the monastery from the financial jurisdiction of the local bishop.[101] If Luther's reforms would have been enacted, the exemptions enjoyed by the monasteries would come to an end and local authorities would once again benefit financially from this new source of revenue through renewed taxation of the land and its resources.

In his fourteenth reform proposal, Luther called for every city to have its own priest and that these priests should be free to marry.[102] The problems of clergy sexual misconduct were well-known during Luther's time. It is believed that Luther consulted canon lawyer Jerome Schurff in order to better understand why priests were prohibited from being married. Finding no adequate answers, he became more and more convinced that the pope had no right to demand clerical celibacy. Though he understood that married priests would need to receive higher wages,

---

97. Ibid., 274.
98. LW 44:169.
99. LW 44:169.
100. LW 44:172f.
101. Lunt, "Financial System," 275.
102. LW 44:175.

he nonetheless believed that married priests would be much less willing to pursue illegitimate sexual relationships.[103]

Luther's fifteenth proposal dealt with the authority of abbots. In monasteries only public sins should be dealt with by the abbot. All other sins should be confessed to fellow priests and monks.[104]

Sixteenth, all masses for the dead should be abolished.[105]

Seventeenth, punishments dictated by canon law, such as the interdict, should be eliminated. This reform proposal also had financial consequences for the papacy. The interdict was one form of punishment used by the papacy to punish those who failed to pay papal taxes. One such example can be found in the case of Elie de Lestrange, bishop of Le Puy, who was one of the prominent figures opposed to papal taxation at the Council of Constance. Upon being appointed as bishop of Saintes, Lestrange realized that eight villages in his diocese had been placed under the papal interdict for failure to pay large debts owed to the papacy.[106] Thus by taking away the right of the papacy to enforce the interdict, Luther was taking away any authority the pope would have to collect revenue from his subjects by threat.

The eighteenth matter to be dealt with concerned festivals in the church calendar. All festivals should be abolished. The only festival day was the celebration of the resurrection on Sundays. The reason for this abolition of festivals was rooted in Luther's realization that the common people are forced to miss work due to festivals and their bodies are weakened when fasts are dictated by the church.[107] Once again, Luther's reforms had a local flavor, as his intention was to free average people from the dictates of a foreign pontiff.

Control over marriages was to become localized in Luther's nineteenth reform proposal. Dispensations for degrees of marriage should come from the local priest, not from Rome.[108]

Twentieth, churches built in fields that served only as pilgrimage sites should be destroyed.[109]

---

103. Brecht, *Road to Reformation*, 373–74.
104. LW 44:180.
105. LW 44:180.
106. Stump, "Reform of Papal Taxation," 83.
107. LW 44:183.
108. LW 44:184.
109. LW 44:185.

Twenty-first, all mendicants and those on pilgrimages should be forbidden to beg for alms or support, in order to discourage the development of mendicant orders and pilgrimages.[110]

Twenty-second, all endowed masses should be abolished.[111]

Twenty-third, brotherhoods and the selling of indulgences should be forbidden.[112]

The issue of brotherhoods, or confraternities, had been taken up by Luther in his 1519 treatise "The Blessed Sacrament of the Holy and True Body of Christ, and the Brotherhoods."[113] When Luther wrote "To the Christian Nobility of the German Nation," there were twenty brotherhoods in Wittenberg.[114]

His arguments against the brotherhoods in 1519 were simple. Luther believed that the brotherhoods were the cause of "gluttony and drunkenness."[115] Men belonging to the brotherhoods used the fraternity as a holy cover for festive living. Luther argued that, if the brotherhoods wish to provide help for the poor, they ought to be fasting and remain sober on feast days. The money they gather should be used for aid to the poor. Specifically, he believed that such money should be used to help people get started in industry rather than giving out unrestricted charity.[116]

Luther identified a spiritual consequence of belonging to brotherhoods. He felt that those belonging to fraternities felt they had a special benefit which applied to members only. "For in them men learn to seek their own good, to love themselves, to be faithful only to one another, to despise others, to think themselves better than others, and to presume to stand higher before God than others."[117] For Luther, the correct understanding of Christian fraternity is to be found in the fellowship of all the saints. As far as organized brotherhoods, they should form a

---

110. LW 44:189.
111. LW 44:191.
112. LW 44:192.
113. LW 35:47–73.
114. LW 44:192 n. 194.
115. LW 35:68.
116. LW 35:69.
117. LW 35:69.

common general fund and give aid to the poor. That alone should be their only task.[118]

Luther had other reasons for attacking the brotherhoods. Though the brotherhoods had been known for their drunkenness, by the sixteenth century they had become a powerful conservative force that stood in the way of reforms that did not originate in Rome. Because brotherhoods were founded as lay mendicant orders, in the beginning of the sixteenth century they were largely under the control of the pope. The task of the brotherhoods has been largely poor relief. Yet with the reform programs offered by Luther and later reformers, the political landscape was changing and the brotherhoods fought to save their control over this area of social life. Luther's reforms specifically called for poor relief to be directed at the deserving poor and for this reason poor laws would be changed, making lay orders irrelevant.[119]

During the late medieval period, poor relief had a decentralized character due in part to mendicant orders and lay orders (such as the brotherhoods). Relief for the poor was at best episodic. It also served as a way of giving a special portion of grace to the giver with little emphasis placed on the recipient of the relief.[120] Luther's demand for the abolition of brotherhoods was in keeping with his understanding that the secular authorities should determine how to meet the needs of the people they rule without the interference of the church authorities. The secularization of poor relief led to a greater emphasis on centralized welfare programs and limited the practice of begging.[121]

Much has been made of Luther's objection to the concept of the selling of forgiveness through indulgences. Yet it is important to highlight that Luther's attack on indulgences was also in keeping with the German *gravamina* and the growing resentment in Germany of the draining of funds away from German to Italy through the sale of indulgences.

By the sixteenth century, indulgences were part of a community's budget. Often the money was used to facilitate special building programs. The construction of St. Ann's church in Annaberg, Saxony was

---

118. LW 35:70–71.

119. Gorski, "Historicising the Secularization Debate," 155.

120. Wright, "Reformation Contributions," D1147–D1148.

121. Ibid., D1158.

paid for through the sale of indulgences. Thus an indulgence acted somewhat like a city bond in twenty-first century North America.[122]

Local leaders usually contributed thirty percent of the income to Rome, which meant that indulgences acted as a sort of revenue sharing program between communities and the Curia. This revenue sharing plan was greeted with more and more skepticism as the anticlerical and anti-Italian sentiments grew in Germany. The resentments turned to outright rebellion as a result of the indulgence that was established to finance Albert of Brandenburg's confirmation fees for his multiple archbishoprics. In addition to the usual fourteen thousand ducat confirmation fee, Albert was forced to pay an additional ten thousand ducats for the honor of serving as archbishop in both Mainz and Magdeburg. In order to pay these fees, Albert sought the permission of the pope to sell an indulgence. Half of the money raised through the sale of the indulgence would be given to Rome for the purpose of building St. Peter's basilica.[123] The Mainz-Magdeburg indulgence was established and the match that would set off the powder keg we have come to call the Reformation was lit.

Albert suspended the sale of all but one other indulgence while his was being sold. Due to the fact that the now suspended indulgences benefited programs and projects in local German communities, while the Mainz-Magdeburg indulgence simply supported an Italian construction program, the revenue-sharing foundation upon which the indulgence sales were built seemed to be crumbling. The impact of this new understanding of indulgences was not missed by the Germans.[124]

By calling for the end of the selling of indulgences, Luther was potentially calling for the end of the revenue-sharing program. This would not only cut into the money that Rome was drawing out of Germany, it practically insured that princes and local authorities would have a new source of taxable income to draw upon because it wasn't being sent voluntarily to Rome anymore! In calling for the end of the indulgence agreement, Luther was drawing upon already existing resentments in Germany concerning the draining of funds away from local communities.

---

122. Kiermayr, "How Much Money," 303.
123. Ibid., 304–7.
124. Ibid., 310.

The twenty-fourth proposal dealt with the question of the Bohemian church and the legacy of John Huss. The question was to be settled by adopting the positions that Huss was killed illegally and that bishops should be sent to Bohemia in order to see to the ordination of proper priests to serve the Bohemian church.[125]

Twenty-fifth, the reform of universities should begin with a call for the faculty to spend less time teaching the methods of Aristotle in order that more time should be spent in the study of scripture.[126]

The twenty-sixth proposal relates directly to our thesis, so it will be examined in some detail. This particular proposal was not part of the first publication of the treatise, but was in place by the time Luther published the second edition. The heart of Luther's argument in this proposal is that the papal curia had, since the time of Charlemagne, claimed to give the Holy Roman Empire to the Germans, and consequently the Germans owe a special debt of gratitude to the pope. Luther's first argument was that the empire had ceased to be after the time of the Goths (410). Yet what was left of the Roman Empire rightly belonged to the emperor in Constantinople. This hereditary office was stolen away by the popes and given to Charlemagne. This "gift" to the Germans was in actuality a trick used by the papacy to control the imperial throne. "Through this we became servants of the pope."[127]

Luther saw the conferring of the title "emperor" on Charlemagne as an historical sham. Luther noted that since the time of Charlemagne the pope has "our wealth, honor, body, life, soul, and all that we possess. This is how they deceive the Germans and cheat us with tricks."[128] Nonetheless, even if the empire had been given to the German people through trickery and deceit, it had indeed been given to the German people. Luther called upon the Germans to take advantage of this fact and take their place as the authority over Rome.

> Now may God, who, as we have said, tossed this empire into our lap by the wiles of tyrants and has charged us with its rule, help us to live up to the name, title, and insignia, and to retrieve our liberty. Let the Romanists see once and for all what it is that we have received from God through them! If they boast that they

---

125. LW 44:196–97.
126. LW 44:201ff.
127. LW 44:206.
128. LW 44:209.

have bestowed an empire on us, let them! If that is true, then let the pope give us back Rome and all that he has gotten from the empire; let him free our land from his intolerable taxing and fleecing; let him give us back our liberty, our rights, our honor, our body and soul; and let the empire be what an empire should be, so that the pope's words and pretensions might be fulfilled.[129]

The notion that the emperor was in the least bit subservient to the pope, because the pope crowned the emperor, was also rejected. Luther's argument was simple: the pope is crowned by three cardinals, but does not submit himself to them. Why then should the emperor go against the example of the pope? Luther's solution to the entire problem was summed up in these words: "Therefore, let the German emperor be really and truly emperor."[130]

The twenty-seventh, and final, reform proposal concerned purely secular matters. Luther called for an end to the extravagant ways that nobles dressed, and he mentions in passing his disdain for the *Zinskauf*. He also called for a restriction of the spice trade, the humbling of the powerful Fugger family, and the curtailing of excessive eating and drinking. Finally he wished for the problems of brothels to be addressed and dealt with.[131]

Of the *Zinskauf* Luther wrote: "If it goes on for another hundred years, Germany will not have a penny left, and the chances are we shall have to eat one another. The devil invented the practice, and by confirming it the pope has brought woe upon the whole world."[132] In fact, Luther labels the *Zinskauf* "the greatest misfortune of the German people."[133]

The *Zinskauf* was a common investment practice in the sixteenth century. By the late Middle Ages money had become the primary method used to pay off a debt. The *Zins* became the way to avoid the ban on usury and operated as a loan contract. Most canonists and theologians considered the *Zinskauf* to be the purchase of the rights to money rather than a loan.[134] Luther considered the *Zinskauf* outright

---

129. LW 44:211.
130. LW 44:212.
131. LW 44:212-14.
132. LW 44:213.
133. LW 44:213.
134. Baker, "Heinrich Bullinger," 51 nn. 7 and 8.

usury.[135] In his February 1520 "Treatise on Good Works," Luther declares, "Third, [the government should] drive out the usurious buying of *tzingskauff* [sic], which brings ruin, trouble, and disaster to every country, every people, and every city by its crafty pretense that it is not usury. They pretend that it is not usury, while in actual fact it is a good deal worse than usury, for men are not on their guard against it as they are against open usury."[136]

The spice trade was another concern of Luther's because he felt that the trade siphoned money away from Germany. He articulates his position in his 1524 treatise, "Trade and Usury": "God has cast us Germans off to such an extent that we have to fling our gold and silver into foreign lands and make the whole world rich, while we ourselves remain beggars. England would have less gold if Germany let her keep her cloth; the king of Portugal would have less if we let him keep his spices."[137] Luther cannot help but make some connection with the *Zinskauf* and the loss of funds through the spice trade. Continuing on with his thoughts on the purchase of spices, Luther writes: "If that hole were stopped up we should not now have to listen to the complaint that there are debts everywhere and no money, that all lands and cities are burdened with *zinss* payments and milked dry by usury."[138]

It seems natural that Luther would pay some attention to the house of the Fuggers as he attacked the practice of lending money. However, the Fuggers also played a prominent role in the system of taxation known as indulgences. During the last half of the fifteenth century, the Fuggers handled most of the indulgence traffic between Rome and the empire. In fact, the Fuggers also operated the papal mint. However, with the arrival of Giovanni de Medici as Pope Leo X on the Roman scene, things changed for the Fuggers. Under Leo X, the Florentine banks regained their power and the right of the Fuggers to control the papal mint was revoked. As a result, the Fuggers had to base most of their financial dealings with the church on the sale of indulgences. They financed the confirmation proceeding of Albert, for which the Mainz-Magdeburg indulgence was established, and actively encouraged the massive increase of the sale of indulgences. Indeed, the Fuggers were

135. Ibid., 51.
136. LW 44:95–96.
137. LW 45:246–47.
138. LW 45:247.

instrumental in securing Albert's confirmation, and helped influence the Vatican to issue the indulgence that was to play so prominent a role in the German Reformation.[139]

Luther ends the treatise by acknowledging the impracticality of his proposals, yet he remains convinced that he has no choice but to take an impractical tone. He fully expected that the treatise itself would come under severe attack. In his final remarks, he remains adamant as to the necessity of his cause. "God give us all a Christian mind, and grant to the Christian nobility of the German nation in particular true spiritual courage to do the best they can for the poor church. Amen."[140]

Some Conclusions

A reading of Luther's reform program reveals several obvious themes: the localization of authority, the end of the pope's authority over secular arenas, and the end of practices which drew money from Germany only to fill papal coffers. In these reforms, one recognizes the grievances of the German people as they had been articulated by those who had for a century presented the *gravamina* to the pope. Additionally, Luther's program influenced future reform proposals, such as the *gravamina* presented to Charles V at the Diet of Worms in 1521, the year following the publication of "To the Christian Nobility of the German Nation."

Like Luther in "To the Christian Nobility of the German Nation," the *gravamina* of 1521 challenged the right of the pope to keep for himself the benefices of those clerics who die in or on the way to Rome.[141] Additionally, in the *gravamina* of 1521, the first grievance is against the transfer of secular cases to Rome, just as in Luther's reform thesis four.[142] The issues of annates and benefices, which Luther so vehemently attacked, were also addressed in 1521 in a variety of formal grievances ranging from the problem of unworthy recipients of benefices and the constant increases in the amounts charged for annates.[143] Just as Luther attacked the practice of reservations, the 1521 *gravamina* sounded off in agreement claiming that the pope never tired in creating new ways

139. Kiermayr, "How Much Money," 308–9.
140. LW 44:217.
141. Strauss, *Manifestations of Discontent*, 54.
142. Ibid., 53.
143. Ibid., 54–55.

of draining money from Germany.[144] The increase of the papal court, which Luther attacked most strongly in thesis seven, was also challenged at Worms because of the high financial burden placed on Germany to pay the court's expenses.[145] Furthermore, those who presented the *gravamina* also objected to papal usurpation of jurisdiction over secular cases, as did Luther in reform thesis four.[146] The presenters of the 1521 *gravamina* also objected to Rome's abuse of pilgrimages as ways of making money for the Roman See, as did Luther in thesis twenty. They demanded twenty-five to thirty-three per cent of all the offerings given by pilgrims at German holy places.[147] Luther and the authors of the 1521 *gravamina* also attacked the constant selling of indulgences. These are only a sampling of the similarities between Luther's reform program and the reforms demanded in the *gravamina* of 1521.

Despite the similarities between Luther's reform program and the *gravamina*, some differences are apparent. To begin, Luther called for a council to solve the religious problems of his day; the *gravamina* of 1521 made no mention of a council. In addition, Luther did not hesitate to attack church authorities, especially the Cardinals, while the *gravamina* of 1521 did not.[148] In Luther's manifesto, the spiritual and the political came together in order to form a complete attack on papal authority. In the *gravamina*, this was not to be the case as only specific issues were addressed without spiritual commentary.[149]

In his work comparing "To the Christian Nobility of the German Nation" to the *gravamina* movement Bruno Gebhardt points out that much of what one finds in Luther's treatise is not original to Luther. Certainly the concept of the universal priesthood is not Luther's invention. Huss and Johannes Wessel had made similar theological claims before Luther's 1520 treatise.[150] And, as stated above, much of the reform programs were also not original to Luther as he borrowed heavily from the traditional *gravamina* of the German clergy.

144. Ibid., 56.
145. LW 44:142 n. 57.
146. LW 44:160 n. 115.
147. LW 44:185 n. 181.
148. Gebhardt, *Die gravamina*, 128.
149. Ibid., 93.
150. Ibid., 127.

What Luther contributed was a theological connection between the concept of the universal priesthood and the demands for reform. In fact, his treatise relies on the universal priesthood as the only foundation upon which the reforms can be carried out. It is for this reason that he structures his treatise as he does. Though some may accuse Luther of being sloppy in his editing,[151] I would argue that the development of his argument is intended to tie political reforms to theological reforms. Only when the walls around the pope have been destroyed with the doctrine of the priesthood of all believers can the political authorities force the church to convene a council independent from the pope, and enact the specific reforms Luther suggests.

The linking of the theological and political reforms in "To the Christian Nobility of the German Nation" is evidence of Luther's intention to articulate evangelical theology in conversation with political realities. This evidence provides the reader with certain knowledge that Luther did not wish to leave the issue of politics to others while he contemplated an otherworldly paradise. In fact, the argument should be made that Luther's theology was at times used by the Reformer for the task of creating a better world.

---

151. Brecht, *Road to Reformation*, 369.

6

Conclusions and Trajectories for Further Studies

WHEN I RETURNED HOME FROM MY TRIP TO GERMANY, I DECIDED TO begin a long journey into Luther's writings. It was my desire, a year into my life as a Lutheran pastor, to reconsider who Luther was and what he was about. Much to my embarrassment, it became obvious to me how little I really knew of Luther from his own words. Most of my encounters with Luther had come through various filters: secondary texts, historical overviews and lectures about Luther. Perhaps if I would have engaged Luther's writings sooner, I would have understood that evangelical theology is not the possession of Germans and Luther is not to be found in Germany. From Luther's own hand, I came to realize that the core of evangelical theology is rooted in encounters with human beings. Luther understood that the way to express the love of God is to be mettlesome; to encounter the world and reflect God's love through love of the neighbor. For Luther, and for those who have adopted his theology, the gospel impacts political reality.

I began my study, as most do, by reading Luther's great 1520 treatises. I was inspired by "The Freedom of a Christian" and bored with "To the Christian Nobility of the German Nation." Twelve years later, I have changed my opinion of Luther's political manifesto to the German nobility and emperor. In its pages I have come to realize how adroit Luther was in his ability to formulate his evangelical doctrine in conversation with the political realities of his day. I am now convinced that in this treatise, Luther has provided a model for how evangelical theology is most properly formulated. Theological reflection is properly done when it considers social structures and seeks to advance the cause of justice. Certainly this is not the only task of theology, yet theology which intentionally ignores any of the orders of creation is insufficient. Luther's understanding of the orders of creation highlight the reality that "the spiritual is not only inwardly, but also outwardly, temporal. The temporal, in turn, is spiritual, insofar as it is the governance of *God on earth*."[1] Luther insisted that the political order was instituted by God. Thus he was able to consider its task in the world and point to ways in which political structures could be reformed, even revolutionized.

In order to make this point, I have engaged in a case study. I chose to concentrate on one aspect of Luther's evangelical doctrine, the doctrine of the universal priesthood. To be more precise, I have chosen to consider Luther's articulation of this doctrine as it was developed in "To the Christian Nobility of the German Nation." I have attempted to demonstrate that Luther's doctrine of the priesthood of all believers is one example of how Luther engaged in a robust attempt to reshape both the ecclesiastical and temporal structures of his day. Despite the common assumptions concerning this doctrine found in the mainstream literature on Luther's life and theology, the universal priesthood cannot be considered exclusively as a doctrine aimed at reforming the structures of the church in regards to the office of ecclesiastical ministry. It must also be considered in light of the political dimensions of the doctrine.

The method I chose to employ was to uncover silences in Luther research. When biographers concluded that Luther's doctrine of the universal priesthood was a doctrine aimed exclusively at redefining the doctrine of ministry, I tested that conclusion. When authors claimed that Luther was not particularly interested in confronting the political structures of his day, I tested that conclusion. Adopting the method of Trouillot, I searched for possibilities that had been rejected by other scholars, and I paid attention to the silences created by those rejections.

I also decided to read Luther through the lens of West's understanding of terms like "political," Christian," "prophetic" and "revolutionary." By adopting these methods and studying the appropriate history through these lenses, I discovered a new and exciting Luther who was very much concerned with reshaping political and temporal structures.

I began testing my assumptions by engaging in a deeper reading of texts I had consulted throughout my years as a student of the Reformation. All but one author included in this study made the claim that when articulating the doctrine of the priesthood of all believers

1. Bayer, "Nature and Institution," 130.

in "To the Christian Nobility of the German Nation," Luther was primarily interested in the reform of the church and its understanding of the office of ministry. Though several authors (Bainton, Oberman, Kittelson and Schwiebert) acknowledged that Luther was interested in the political realities of his day, Schwiebert alone insists that the priesthood of all believers was part of Luther's reform program for the secular realm. Other authors share Schwiebert's view, yet they exist outside the mainstream voices which serve to set the boundaries of discussion concerning Luther's life and thought. Bainton, Kittelson and Oberman see only accidental connections between the universal priesthood and the reforms of secular society that Luther advocated. Brecht, Lohse and Marius completely dismiss the possibility that the universal priesthood was used by Luther to provide a new vision of both the church and the temporal powers.

Lohse concludes that the important part of "To the Christian Nobility of the German Nation" is to be found in the theological portions of the text, not the program for reform of the secular powers. This implies that the theological foundation of the texts can be separated from Luther's advocacy in the treatise for secular and ecclesial reforms. Though Lohse certainly comprehends the political implications of Luther's thought, it is my contention that he does not fully explore the source of Luther's political thought. Brecht makes the bold assertion that Luther was never interested in making changes in the secular realms of life.

Each of these authors is correct when they conclude that Luther intended his doctrine of the universal priesthood to be understood as an evangelical understanding of the doctrine of ministry. I have demonstrated that throughout his career Luther was clear that the universal priesthood was a theological insight that would impact the task of ministry. Indeed, I have shown in my examination of Luther's writings that his "To the Christian Nobility of the German Nation" treats the concept of the universal priesthood in a unique way when he lifts up the political dimensions of the text. In my opinion, it is this unique presentation of the universal priesthood in "To the Christian Nobility of the German Nation" that is so compelling. The uniqueness of Luther's articulation of the doctrine in this treatise allows the political dimensions of the theology to stand in stark contrast to his other works on the same topic.

By examining how Luther articulated the doctrine of the universal priesthood throughout his career, the reader recognizes some patterns developing in his thought. First, the notion of the universal priesthood stands as a direct attack on the authority of the pope. Yet, one can also recognize that Luther is not advocating a kind of grassroots democracy in which there is no distinction between peoples or the offices they hold. Thus, the ministry of the ordained must be controlled and limited. The holder of the office of ministry is to be a servant. If the officeholder is unable to meet this requirement then that person is to be replaced.

As I showed in my research, his early commentary on Romans 3 revealed a traditional understanding of the priesthood. By 1520, in his "Treatise on the New Testament" and "Babylonian Captivity of the Church," the issue at stake for Luther was the sacramental nature of Roman ordination. In these texts, along with "The Misuse of the Mass" and "Concerning the Ministry," Luther claims that ordination cannot be understood sacramentally. In "The Freedom of a Christian" Luther's universal priesthood stands as a call for a renewed commitment to Christian life. In his polemics against Emser, "Defense and Explanation of All the Articles," "Misuse of the Mass," commentary on 1 Peter, commentary on Isaiah and commentary on Psalm 110, Luther uses the universal priesthood as a way of discussing the office of the ministry. In his work with the community of Leisnig, the universal priesthood was a sign of Christian freedom in regards to calling pastors. While exegeting Psalm 45, Luther expounded upon how the universal priesthood impacts the doctrine of justification. He also took an opportunity to take an additional shot at papal authority. In his sermon at Torgau, Luther once again used the universal priesthood as a call for renewal in Christian life and a commitment to the doctrine of Christian freedom.

It is also interesting to note that at times the doctrine of the universal priesthood is used as a tool for understanding—or influencing—the political realm. This is the case in "Dr. Luther's Retraction," in which Luther accuses Emser and the papists of fearing a inevitable loss of temporal power if the Roman priesthood is eliminated. In "The Misuse of the Mass," Luther is aware of the reality that the rights of bishops and priests to the properties they control would change or disappear if the priesthood is universal. In his work with the congregation at Leisnig, Luther is working directly with secular authorities in order to help them break away from the Roman church. As justification for their action, the community recalls its universal priesthood and thus takes back its right to choose who will serve as spiritual leader in the community church. In his commentary on Psalm 82, the universal priesthood is invoked as a reminder to temporal authorities that they must control abuses in the church. Again, in "Concerning the Ministry" Luther is directly dealing with the Senate in Prague and uses the universal priesthood as a justification for that community to remain rebellious in the face of the demands of the pope.

The unique quality of Luther's "To the Christian Nobility of the German Nation" can best be understood by a deeper examination of the historical, theological and political issues that created the need for Luther to attack the primacy of the pope. Though Luther was not the first to challenge the appropriateness of the pope's actions, he was among the first to significantly challenge the fundamental nature of papal power. In so doing he did not simply attack temporal or political structures, he attempted to destroy the cosmology of his day.

Papal authority in the Middle Ages, as I demonstrated in the fourth chapter, was based on a cosmological understanding of God's will for the created order and rested on a strict division between laity and clergy. Medieval cosmology understood the cosmos as a reflection of the body of Christ, as understood by Paul. There are the head and members, all of which exist to serve the kingdom of God. The doctrines of the day held that the sacred dimensions of the body, rooted in the authority of the pope as Vicar of Christ on earth, possess ultimate power (*principatus*), which granted them ultimate authority to order the structures of the world (*auctoritas*). This power and authority was shared with the temporal powers in order to free the church from such tasks as presiding over criminal trials and determining how to punish criminals. The temporal authorities are given by the pope the ability to carry out administrative functions (*potestas*). Though temporal authorities tried many times to challenge the terms by which the church exercised authority, they rarely challenged the nature of the authority of the pope rooted in the cosmology of the day.

Several documents reveal the church's understanding of its authority over the temporal sphere. Both the "Donation of Constantine" and *Unam Sanctam* provide ample evidence of the ways in which the church understood its role as lord of all things on earth. Though the "Donation" was eventually proved to be a forgery, the document certainly had a significant impact on the ways papal authority was exercised in the Middle Ages. The document made the claim that the Emperor Constantine granted that the pope was lord of all things in the empire and was to be recognized as the sole ruler of the church. *Unam Sanctam* solidified this authority in its claim that the one true church was led by one pope in Rome. The pope possessed both the temporal and spiritual swords and permitted temporal authorities to wield power on the pope's terms.

Luther's challenge to this cosmology was most directly articulated in "To the Christian Nobility of the German Nation." In this treatise, Luther responds to the political realities of his day in light of his doctrine of justification. He fully understood the traditions behind the "Donation" and *Unam Sanctam*. He was also aware of the variety of ways that medieval cosmology propagated by these documents had placed the papacy above reform. Thus relying on evangelical doctrine, Luther challenged the very foundations of papal authority by claiming that there is no division between lay and cleric in the realms of estate. All baptized Christians are priests and have been provided vocations which advance the cause of the gospel.

Luther focuses on the divinely instituted task of leading civil governments and makes the claim that temporal government exists to protect the people of God and the universal church. If the structures of the church begin to act contrary to God's will, it is up to the civil authorities to fulfill their priestly roles as reformers of the church and protector of evangelical doctrine.

With this theological insight, Luther shatters medieval cosmology at its core. By denying the fundamental separation of lay and cleric, he has attacked the root of both the ecclesiastical and temporal realms as they were understood in the sixteenth century.

Drawing on the reform movements that preceded him, armed with a new cosmology, Luther demanded that the temporal authorities convene a council to see to proper church reform. He drew upon the traditional *gravamina* of the German nation as he proposed a reform program that would impact the temporal and spiritual structures in the empire.

As stated at the outset of this case study, the purpose of this work is to engage in a case study which can inform modern thinkers concerning the intention of Martin Luther in creating a new and alternative understanding of the role and authority of those in positions of temporal power. As moderns, we may never know Luther's intentions, but we can test assumptions about his motivations by examining what he said in light of different assumptions. Our assumption has been that Luther was interested in radically changing the political structures of his day. We have tested this assumption by examining the history of authority in the Middle Ages and the papacy in the early modern period. We have then considered how these historical realities impacted Luther's writings, in this particular case study we have focused on "To the Christian Nobility of the German Nation."

From such an examination, we have discovered that Luther most certainly had in mind a new vision for how temporal authority and the structures of this authority should be made manifest in the world. This discovery contradicts a great many scholars who have concluded that Luther was not particularly interested in worldly matters, with the exception of the "doctrine" of two governances. Indeed, the ability to understand the fullness of Luther's conception of politics and temporal authority has been undermined by assumptions of Luther's unwillingness to engage in reshaping political realities. By engaging in this case study, we have identified a silence in Luther historiography which has at best clouded the understanding of students of Luther concerning his political thought and, at worst, has perpetuated a false understanding of Luther and Lutheran theology as quietistic and uninterested in temporal ethical thought and action.

Moving Forward: Implications for the Political Dimensions of the Universal Priesthood

What was silenced, the political dimensions of the universal priesthood, has been given voice. The descriptions of Luther during the last century that we have studied sought to present the man based on the available information, in a way that would allow modern readers to better understand his impact and influence on history. Yet how can we in a modern age comprehend the life and work of a medieval and early modern man?

Terms and concepts like conservative are used to describe Luther even though the term is loaded with contextual significance for the person studied and the student who is separated from the historical figure by centuries.[2] But perhaps these sorts of labels are necessary if we are ever going to attempt the task of considering the life and legacy of any historical figure. The labels, while inadequate, may be useful.

In the light of the research presented, I would like to present alternative labels to describe Luther's political thought. My own labels will be no more adequate than the ones used by any other scholar who attempts to bridge the centuries through conceptual means like language. Yet my labels will be based on information gleaned directly from the writings of Luther and a thorough examination of the contexts surrounding and undergirding the document "To the Christian Nobility of the German Nation."

Utilizing definitions provided by Cornel West, I suggest that Luther's thought, especially as it was applied to the universal priesthood in 1520, can be described as political, prophetic, revolutionary, and Christian.

We recall that the term "political" is defined by West as an "attempt to enrich and enable the struggle for freedom."[3] Taken this way, any attempt at setting people free from structures that reduce the potential of freedom is a political struggle. Even if one were to conclude that Luther was interested only in the matters of the spirit, the fact that his was a struggle for liberation of the Christian from the bonds of the papacy should be understood as a political act. Yet it can and should be argued that the church as the locus of the spiritual world in the Middle Ages included all of creation. This cosmology placed all things temporal and political into the realm of the spirit. The temporal world was consumed by the spiritual world and temporal matters were not considered to have any independent value outside their connection to the church. Therefore, Luther's battles for freedom in the realm of the spiritual life of people were fundamentally impacted by the temporal world. Yet, Luther did more than simply address matters of the spirit. He utilized spiritual doctrines to conceptually liberate the temporal world from the control of the church and thus reconstructed the concept and structures of temporal authority. By West's definition, Luther's evangelical theology, especially as it was articulated in "To the Christian Nobility

---

2. See especially Bainton, *Here I Stand*, 232; Brecht, *Road to Reformation*, 375; and Lohse, *Introduction*, 51.

3. West, *Prophesy Deliverance*, 5.

of the German Nation" in the form of the universal priesthood, was a political theology.

West defines "prophecy" as the identification of concrete evils. "To prophesy is not to predict an outcome but rather to identify concrete evils. To prophesy deliverance is not to call for some otherworldly paradise but rather to generate enough faith, hope, and love to sustain the human possibility for more freedom."[4] I am certainly not foolish enough to suggest that Luther would have personally espoused all the claims made by West concerning the definition of prophesy. Luther, unlike West, was happy to contemplate an otherworldly paradise. Yet those who study Luther recognize in his universal priesthood a direct attack on what he considered to be a concrete evil—the Roman understanding of the priesthood and its power rooted in the papacy. His call for all Christians to consider themselves priests and inheritors of God's power to forgive in Jesus Christ, freed the individual Christian from obedience to the ordained priesthood in temporal matters. He utilized no weapons other than the weak armor of scripture and tradition, to borrow language from West, to make his claim and had no illusion that his perspective would achieve any worldly acceptance.[5] This final point leads us to consider West's definition of a revolutionary.

West believes that the task of a revolutionary thinker is "to transform abstract talk about God and suffering into concrete enactments of existential and political struggles with no human guarantee for ultimate victory."[6] Luther's call for the political authorities to discipline the pope and understand themselves as priests capable of reforming the church was a concrete act of defiance. Furthermore, Luther provided twenty-seven proposals for restructuring the system of papal taxation, establishing local authority, and seeing an end to practices which would place average German people under the thumb of a foreign pope. Yet Luther held no illusions that his plan for reform would be received by those in authority. Assuming the role of the court jester, Luther informs his friend, Nicholas von Amsdorf, "Perhaps I owe my God and the world another work of folly. I intend to pay my debt honestly. And if I succeed,

---

4. West, *Prophesy Deliverance*, 6.

5. See LW 44:123; 216–17. Certainly Luther did not believe that Scripture was weak armor. Yet he understood that the powers of the world are at time unmoved by the Word of God.

6. West, *Prophesy Deliverance*, 6.

I shall for the time being become a court jester. And if I fail, I still have one advantage—no one need buy me a cap or put scissors to my head."[7] In the final paragraphs of his treatise he remarks, "I know full well that I have been very outspoken. I have made many suggestions that will be considered impractical. I have attacked many things too severely."[8]

Finally, in a case study such as this West's definition of the concept of the "Christian" could fuel an interesting discussion concerning the type of Christian Luther was. West defines the term "Christian" in the context of his definitions of politics, prophecy, and revolution. In order to turn the concepts into meaningful descriptors of types of actions, he attaches them to an agent—the Christian person who confronts "the darker sides, and the human plights, of societies and souls with the weak armor of compassion and justice." Certainly this is the type of Christianity exemplified by Luther in "To the Christian Nobility of the German Nation" as he leveled his attack against the papacy.

A Christian is a political person when he or she seeks to enrich and enable the struggle for freedom, not simply temporal freedom, but the freedom to live in dignity and peace. One recognizes that the search for Christian freedom was essential to Luther throughout 1520. In his address to the nobility Luther proposed concrete ways in which to rid Germany of the oppressive theology that under-girded an oppressive system of taxation.

A Christian is a prophet when he or she works to identify concrete evils in the world. This is exactly what Luther does in "To the Christian Nobility of the German Nation." He does not simply rail against the Roman priesthood. He identifies how the pope uses the priesthood as a means of defending what Luther considered an oppressive system.

A Christian is a revolutionary when he or she transforms theology into concrete acts of engagement with evil. Equipped only with compassion and justice (presumably rooted in the person of Christ, though West is less than adamant about this particular point), informed by what West calls "my Marxist heritage," he goes on to proclaim that the political, prophetic, and revolutionary Christian lives in the hope of new life lived in "revolutionary patience in the face of an ice age that aborts any immediate chance for fundamental social change."[9] Undeterred

7. LW 44:123.
8. LW 44:216–17.
9. West, *Prophesy Deliverance*, 8.

by the possibility that his reforms would be ignored Luther makes his claim and hopes those in authority will answer his call for reform. Thus, Luther was a political, prophetic and revolutionary Christian.

A Trajectory for Further Study

A trajectory for future study would be to further explore how political issues played a role in pushing the Reformer into articulating evangelical doctrine. By moving beyond this single case study, utilizing the methods found in these pages, such studies may in fact reveal the close connection between church and state in the development of Reformation doctrine so that contemporary historians and theologians will be empowered to understand the intimate connection between contemporary theology and contemporary politics. Additionally, the revolutionary and prophetic aspects of Luther's theology, as understood through the lens of West's definitions, will provide a new understanding of Luther which may override the assumptions that Luther's theology was conservative of the quietist variety in matters temporal and political.

Additionally, it would be interesting to examine the "doctrine" of two kingdoms as it relates to the universal priesthood in order to better understand why Luther wrote what he did about the left- and right-hand kingdoms in his treatise "Temporal Authority." That document was written as a supplement to "To the Christian Nobility of the German Nation." Linking those two documents to one another for the express purpose of examining the link between the universal priesthood and the two governances will certainly provide fertile soil for future work.

The question of Luther's cosmology will also need further study. After exploring how Luther dismantled the medieval cosmology with his universal priesthood for the sake of structural reform in the church and state, it remains to be seen how exactly Luther would re-envision the idea of the cosmic order. As it was suggested in chapter five, the new work being done on the orders of creation will perhaps provide the best answer to this question.

Finally, as a result of my research, it is clear that the *gravamina* and the movement around the grievances are often cited as having a significant impact on Luther's thought. However, there is almost no current research on the *gravamina*, and there is essentially no significant research in English. Translations of the work done by Bruno Gebhardt would serve students of the Reformation well. In addition, translations of primary documents are needed if there is to be a more significant understanding of the medieval antecedents of the reform proposals articulated by Luther among those who study Luther in English.

The primary task of this case study has been accomplished. The purpose of this work is to call into question the assumption that Luther was not a political visionary. The silences created by mainstream biographers have been identified. A new image of Luther has been presented through an examination of Luther's doctrine of the universal priesthood as articulated in "To the Christian Nobility of the German Nation." I have presented a lens through which one may view a new image of Luther. This image highlights the visionary and political aspects of Luther's evangelical theology. The lens was borrowed from another visionary, Cornel West. Yet this lens has been applied to only one aspect of Luther's evangelical theology. This case study is limited by definition. The work that remains is to apply this lens to other doctrines and texts in order to understand the political dimensions of Luther's gospel beyond the doctrine of the priesthood of all believers.

Bibliography

Altmann, Walter. *Luther and Liberation: A Latin American Perspective.* Minneapolis: Fortress, 1992.
Bainton, Roland. *Here I Stand: A Life of Martin Luther.* New York: Abingdon, 1950.
Baker, J. Wayne. "Heinrich Bullinger and the Idea of Usury." *Sixteenth Century Journal* 5 (1974) 49–70.
Barth, Hans-Martin. *Einander Priester sein: Allgemeines Priestertum in ökumenischer Perspektive.* Göttingen: Vandenhoeck & Ruprecht, 1990.
Bayer, Oswald. "Nature and Institution." *Lutheran Quarterly* 12 (Summer 1998) 125–59.
Bellitto, Christopher M. *The General Councils: A History of the Twenty-One Church Councils from Nicaea to Vatican II.* New York: Paulist, 2002.
Braaten, Carl, and Robert W. Jenson, editors. *Christian Dogmatics.* 2 vols. Philadelphia: Fortress, 1984.
Brecht, Martin. *Martin Luther: His Road to Reformation, 1483–1521.* Translated by James L. Schaaf. Philadelphia: Fortress, 1985.
Brendler, Gerhard. *Martin Luther: Theology and Revolution.* Translated by Claude R. Foster Jr. New York: Oxford University Press, 1991.
Brunotte, Heinz. *Das Amt der Verkündigung und das Priestertum aller Gläubigen.* Berlin: Lutherisches Verlagshaus, 1962.
Davis, Leo Donald. *The First Seven Ecumenical Councils (325–787): Their History and Theology.* Collegeville, MN: Liturgical, 1983.
Druckenbrod, Wolfgang. *Das Verständnis des allgemeinen Priestertums im 19. und 20. Jahrhundert.* Bad Honnef: Bock & Herchen, 1979.
Dyson, R. W. *Normative Theories of Society and Government in Five Medieval Thinkers: St. Augustine, John of Salisbury, Giles of Rome, St. Thomas Aquinas, and Marsilius of Padua.* Medieval Studies, Volume 21. Lewiston, NY: Mellen, 2003.
Eastwood, Cyril. *The Priesthood of All Believers: An Examination of the Doctrine from the Reformation to the Present Day.* Minneapolis: Augsburg, 1960.
———. *The Royal Priesthood of the Faithful: An Investigation of the Doctrine from Biblical Times to the Reformation.* Minneapolis: Augsburg, 1963.
Fragnito, Gigliola. "Cardinals' Courts in Sixteenth-Century Rome." *Journal of Modern History* 65 (1993) 26–56.
Frequens, Medieval Sourcebook. Fordham University. Online: http://www.fordham.edu/halsall/source/constance2.html.
Fuchs, Ralf-Peter. "The Supreme Court of the Holy Roman Empire: The State of Research and the Outlook." *Sixteenth Century Journal* 34 (2003) 9–27.
Gebhardt, Bruno. *Die gravamina der Deutschen Nation gegen den römischen Hof.* Breslau: Koebner, 1895.

Giles, Edward, editor. *Documents Illustrating Papal Authority, A.D. 96–454*. London: SPCK, 1952.
Goertz, Harald. *Allgemeines Priestertum und Ordiniertes Amt bei Luther*. Marburg: Elwert, 1997.
Gonzalez, Justo. *The Story of Christianity: Volume 1, The Early Church to the Dawn of the Reformation*. San Francisco: HarperSanFrancsico, 1984.
Gorski, Philip S. "Historicising the Secularization Debate: Church, State, and Society in Late Medieval and Early Modern Europe, ca. 1300-1700." *American Sociological Review* 65 (2000) 138–67. (Looking Forward, Looking Back: Continuity and Change at the Turn of the Millenium [sic]).
Grimm, Harold. *The Reformation Era, 1500–1650*. New York: Macmillan, 1965.
Gritsch, Eric W. *A History of Lutheranism*. Minneapolis: Fortress, 2002.
Harrisville, Roy A. *Ministry in Crisis: Changing Perspectives on Ordination and the Priesthood of All Believers*. Minneapolis: Augsburg, 1987.
Henderson, Ernest F. *Select Historical Documents of the Middle Ages*. London: Bell, 1910.
Hendrix, Scott. *Luther and the Papacy: Stages in a Reformation Conflict*. Philadelphia: Fortress, 1981.
Hutten, Ulrich von. *Ulrichs von Hutten Schriften*. Vol. 5. Edited by Eduard Röcking. Aalen: Zeller, 1963.
Keen, Ralph. *Divine and Human Authority in Reformation Thought: German Theologians on Political Order 1520–1555*. Nieuwkoop: De Graaf, 1997.
Kiermayr, Reinhold. "How Much Money was Actually in the Indulgence Chest?" *Sixteenth Century Journal* 17 (1986) 303–18.
Kittelson, James M. *Luther the Reformer: The Story of the Man and His Career*. Minneapolis: Augsburg, 1986.
Kolb, Robert, and Timothy Wengert, editors. *The Book of Concord*. Minneapolis: Fortress, 2000.
Lau, Franz, and Ernst Bizer. *A History of the Reformation in Germany to 1555*. London: Adam & Charles Black, 1969.
Lieberg, Hellmut. *Amt und Ordination bei Luther und Melanchthon*. Göttingen: Vandenhoeck & Ruprecht, 1962.
Lohse, Bernhard. *Martin Luther: An Introduction to His Life and Work*. Translated by Robert C. Schultz. Philadelphia: Fortress, 1986.
———. *Martin Luther's Theology*. Translated and edited by Roy A. Harrisville. Minneapolis: Fortress, 1999.
Lunt, W. E. "The Financial System of the Medieval Papacy in the Light of Recent Literature." *Quarterly Journal of Economics* 23 (1909) 251–95.
Luscombe, David. "The '*Lex Divinitatis*' in the Bull '*Unam Sanctam*' of Pope Boniface VIII." In *Church and Government in the Middle Ages*, edited by C. N. L. Brooke, D. E. Luscombe et al. Cambridge: Cambridge University Press, 1976.
Luther, Martin. *D. Martin Luthers Werke: Kristische Gesamtausgabe*. Edited by J. K. F. Knaake, G. Kawerau, et al., 58 vols. Weimar: Böhlau, 1883–.
———. *Luther's Works*. Edited by Jaroslav Pelikan, vols. 1–30, and Helmut T. Lehmann, vols. 31–55. Philadelphia: Fortress; St. Louis: Concordia, 1955–1986.
Lytle, Guy Fitch, editor. *Reform and Authority in the Medieval and Reformation Church*. Washington, DC: Catholic University of America Press, 1981.

Mackinnon, James. *Luther and the Reformation: Volume II The Breach with Rome (1517–21)*. New York: Longmans, Green, 1928.
Marius, Richard. *Martin Luther: The Christian Between God and Death*. Cambridge, MA: Belknap, 1989.
Marty, Martin. *Martin Luther*. New York: Penguin, 2004.
McCready, William D. "Papal Plenitudo Potestatis and the Source of Temporal Authority in Late Medieval Papal Hierocratic Theory." *Speculum* 48 (1973) 654–74.
Oberman, Heiko A. *Luther: Man between God and the Devil*. Translated by Eileen Walliser-Schwarzbart. New Haven: Yale University Press, 1989.
Paquette, Robert L. Review of *Silencing the Past: Power and the Production of History*, by Michel-Rolph Trouillot. *Journal of American History* 84 (1997) 189–90.
Pelikan, Jaroslav. *Reformation of the Church and Dogma (1300-1700)*. Chicago: University of Chicago Press, 1984.
Pope Boniface VIII. "*Unam Sanctam.*" In *Medieval Sourcebook*. Fordham University. Online: http://www.fordham.edu/halsall/source/b8-unam.html.
Pope Pius II. "*Execrabilis.*" In *Medieval Sourcebook*. Fordham University. Online: http://www.fordham.edu/halsall/source/p2-execrabilis.html.
Postan, M. M., editor. *The Cambridge Economic History of Europe*. Vol. 3, *Economic Organization and Policies in the Middle Ages*. Cambridge: Cambridge University Press, 1965.
Preus, Herman A. "Luther on the Universal Priesthood and the Office of the Ministry." *Concordia Journal* 5.2 (1979) 55–62.
Reinhart, Max, editor. *Infinite Boundaries: Order, Disorder, and Reorder in Early Modern German Culture*. Kirksville, MO: Sixteenth Century Journal Publishers, 1998.
Rich, E. E., and C. H. Wilson, editors. *The Cambridge Economic History of Europe*. Vol. IV, *The Economy of Expanding Europe in the Sixteenth and Seventeenth Centuries*. Cambridge: Cambridge University Press, 1967.
Rogge, Joachim. *Anfänge der Reformation: Der junge Luther 1483-1521, Der junge Zwingli 1484-1523*. Berlin: Evangelische Verlagsanstalt, 1985.
Schilling, Heinz. *Religion, Political Culture and the Emergence of Early Modern Society: Essays in German and Dutch History*. New York: Brill, 1992.
Schwarz, Hans. *True Faith in the True God: An Introduction to Luther's Life and Thought*. Translated by Mark William Worthing. Minneapolis: Augsburg, 1996.
Schwiebert, Ernest G. *Luther and His Times: The Reformation From a New Perspective*. St. Louis: Concordia, 1950.
———. "The Medieval Pattern in Luther's Views of the State." *Church History* 12.2 (1943) 98–117.
Spinka, Matthew, translator. *John Hus at the Council of Constance*. New York: Columbia University Press, 1965.
Spitz, L. W. "The Universal Priesthood of Believers with Luther's Comments." *Concordia Theological Monthly* 23 (January 1952) 1–15.
Storck, Hans. *Das allgemeine Priestertum bei Luther*. Munich: Kaiser, 1953.
Strauss, Gerald, editor and translator. *Manifestations of Discontent in Germany on the Eve of the Reformation*. Bloomington: Indiana University Press, 1971.
Stump, Phillip H. "The Reform of Papal Taxation at the Council of Constance (1414–1418)." *Speculum* 64 (1989) 69–105.

Sweet, Alfred H. "Papal Privileges Granted to Individual Religious." *Speculum* 31 (1956) 602–10.

Tavard, George H. "The Bull Unam Sanctam of Boniface VIII." In *Papal Primacy and the Universal Church*. Edited by P. C. Empie and A. T. Murphy. Minneapolis: Augsburg, 1974.

Tellenbach, Gerd. *Church, State and the Christian Society at the Time of the Investiture Contest*. Translated by R. F. Bennett. Oxford: Blackwell, 1966.

Toiviainen, Kalevi. "Holiness, Sanctification and the Saints Especially from the Standpoint of the Universal Priesthood." *Mikkeli* (1986) 20-39.

Trouillot, Michel-Rolph. *Silencing the Past: Power and the Production of History*. Boston: Beacon, 1995.

Ullmann, Walter, "Boniface VIII and His Contemporary Scholarship." *Journal of Theological Studies* 27 (1976) 58–87.

———. *Growth of Papal Government in the Middle Ages*. London: Methuen, 1962.

Valla, Lorenzo. *The Treatise of Lorenzo Valla on the Donation of Constantine*. Translated by Christopher B. Coleman. Toronto: University of Toronto Press, 1993.

Watanabe, Morimichi. "The Episcopal Election of 1430 in Trier and Nicholas of Cusa." *Church History* 39 (1970) 299–316.

West, Cornel. *Prophesy Deliverance! An Afro-American Revolutionary Christianity*. Louisville: Westminster John Knox, 2002.

Williams, George. *The Norman Anonymous of 1100 A.D.* Harvard Theological Studies 18. Cambridge: Harvard University Press, 1951.

Wright, William. "Reformation Contributions to the Development of Public Welfare Policy in Hesse." *Journal of Modern History* 49 On Demand Supplement (June 1977) D1145–D1179.

www.ingramcontent.com/pod-product-compliance
Lightning Source LLC
Chambersburg PA
CBHW051940160426
43198CB00013B/2236